RE-MEMORIES
of a Disgraced Police Chief

HARV SIMMONS

ISBN: 1456386530
ISBN-13: 9781456386535

ACKNOWLEDGMENTS

This book could not have been written without the love and devotion and many hours of editing from my wife Dianne. As in my life, she is the one that makes me go and keeps me going. A special thanks to my good friend Dr. Jim Brown whose past as a top notch educator put the book in proper form and perspective. The encouragement from his opinion of the first few chapters made a huge difference in my attitude when I asked,

"Well Jim, what do you think?"

He looked up from the table and stared directly into my face and said,

"Wow!"

He added, "This should be a movie."

PROLOGUE

I had seen my share of life in my thirty six years; witnessing death, sorrow, happiness, loneliness, togetherness, belonging and not belonging.

I appreciated every part of my life and time in law enforcement. Yet, I was very confused by my present circumstances. I have never been able to believe or accept what happened. But it did happen and it wasn't pretty.

In a single day in 1972 I was fired in one courtroom, indicted for extortion in another, divorced in a family court and refused to testify against my assailant in a district court in the afternoon.

This is my story and the events that led me to that traumatic day in court.

To the best of my recollection and through saved newspaper articles and court documents everything in this book is the truth. Nothing has been embellished or stretched to sound more entertaining (if that could be the case). There are parts of the book I did not particularly like, but to change or alter the meaning would have meant I altered the truth and I refused to do that. If there are some hurt feelings to the families I have named I apologize to those families. I do not apologize to subjects involved.

This book, the story, will take a lot of twists and turns but I have tried hard not to confuse anyone or lose you along the way. There have been times when I literally felt the pain and heartbreak all over again, tears actually rolled down my cheeks.

A good portion of the story was written nearly forty years ago. I never did anything much with it because a number of people had me convinced I was either going to be sued, assassinated or maybe both.

Some of you will remember Eddie Egan, the former New York City detective who wrote and starred in the movie The French Connection. To make a long story short, he and my wife and I met one evening and got talking about being former cops and his movie. I told him about my book. The following morning he was at my apartment asking for my copy and could he borrow it? Being green and naïve to this part of Hollywood I gave it to him. We didn't see Egan again for weeks. I got suspicious and to make a long story short we located him through his agent who ordered him to bring the book back. He did and we discovered that he was "shopping the book around" to make a movie out of it. Obviously he thought the book had some potential.

Why did I finish the book now? This is a story of a lot of men and women who have been abused by dirty politics. There were lawyers, doctors, specialists or trades people all looking for more and more power and personal privilege. All at a cost to the good people who trusted them to do the right thing. The truth is it has never been about the "good people" and probably never will be. It's called politics and there is no good side to that.

In my book, I comment on one very unfortunate incident where a small neighbor girl lost most of her arm in a lawn mower accident. The main concern on that afternoon was how long it took the local cops to get to the scene of the accident and how inept they were. You will read that I made a comment about one day becoming the chief of police and changing the perception of the police department. My absolute and sincere purpose for accepting the position as chief of police was to give the people a department they could be proud of and what they deserved.

I did give the community a good solid and honest police department. I didn't count on what happened four months after I was appointed.

How we got through our bad times will probably always be fodder for debate. A group of dedicated gentleman, ladies and volunteers, gave everything they had and turned the Coventry, Rhode Island police department into one excellent protective crime fighting agency. I could not have asked more from them. The citizens responded wonderfully well.

* * *

As you will notice in the acknowledgements, my wife had a huge hand in making this book possible. Dianne mentioned something to me toward the end of the book that I certainly didn't realize or even think of.

She said to me, "You know, if I didn't know you, or what happened, in advance of this book, I would think you were extremely confident with your abilities but came off, at times, as being cocky".

To say the least, I was taken aback. Actually, it was more like I got whacked over the head with one of those cast iron frying pans. After a moment or two, (hours actually) I realized she was right. I hate it when she's right. I say this with the most profound amount of honesty. If that is the way the reader visualizes me, I sincerely apologize. It is not intended.

There is no way to explain the amount of work, preparation, investigation and digging it takes to substantiate facts and comments made in this book. Writing was relatively easy. I tried to write as though I was talking to a group of friends. Over the years many of those friends have heard the stories. The editing and re-writes were a real wake up call. I have heard many tales of woe from other writers, but I just fluffed them off and plodded ahead. Maybe someday I will learn to listen.

In the final analysis, I am a lot older and wiser now, but my passion for what I undertook and was able to do still burns in my soul.

My wife and I have owned and sold three businesses. We have done quite well and are now retired. I even got into politics and served six years as a county supervisor and was elected chairman of a twenty- eight member board. I also served on the local school board.

Dianne and I have accomplished a lot. Our lives together turned out very well. We're happy. We've made some wonderful friends.

For many years I wanted to make a formal apology to friends and relatives back in Rhode Island because I felt I let them down. In the summer of 2010 I had that opportunity at a high school class reunion and addressed my concerns to those present at the affair. I was told by numerous classmates it wasn't necessary to apologize. They never lost faith in me. Pretty cool bunch, the Class of 1953.

In the years since I was fired, I have realized that I, indeed, planted some seeds back in the community. From what I understand members of the Coventry Police department can be proud of who they are and what they continue to do. I know I am.

That's why I wrote this book. Enjoy!

RE-MEMORIES

PART ONE

CHAPTER 1

It would be extremely difficult for anyone to understand the complexities of the time period that this story encompasses. I could not understand what happened to me, or how or why I had become involved in such a political and personal mess. It seemed like I had no control over the circumstances and certainly not the outcome.

I was born in the neighboring town of West Warwick, Rhode Island. I lived with my two older brothers and of course my mother. We lived in a six family tenement house. The neighborhood consisted of Italians, Portuguese, Germans, Irish and was a melting pot as were many other sections of the town of West Warwick.

When I was eleven, my mother bought our first home in Coventry, Rhode Island.

Coventry is in the west-central portion of the state and extends to the eastern Connecticut state line. The township with a population of approximately 25,000 was mostly rural.

Although Rhode Island is the smallest state in the union, Coventry has the distinction of being the largest town area-wise in the United States with more than three hundred miles of roads.

In 1949 one of my best neighborhood friends, Bobby Carlson, told me the Coventry police were going to start a junior police department and a meeting was going to be held at the police station/town hall complex. I agreed to go to the meeting with Bobby thinking what a thrill it would be to be able to work alongside police officers. We joined the junior police and small tin badges were passed out to those of us who took a simple little examination to pass the safety course. As I recall we all passed, all twelve of us.

I was given badge number one. Ironic isn't it? Twenty years later, at 33, I would come back and once again be given badge number one; this time, as the chief of police.

In the mid nineteen fifties the Korean War was raging. Two days after graduation from Coventry high school I joined the Marine Corps and was at Parris Island shortly after training for combat in Korea.

After discharge from the Marine Corps I worked at several menial jobs. One late afternoon I walked into my mother's home. She was reading an advertisement in the local newspaper.

Mom said, "The state police are looking for men, why don't you go and apply?"

"I didn't know they lost any." I really had no desire to be a beat cop walking around town shaking doors.

Millie, my loving name for Mom, said "I don't think state troopers do that."

She was right. I decided to take her advice and applied. There were more than Six hundred fifty candidates. Twenty-three men were selected to attend the state police academy and seventeen of us graduated with my class.

My class graduated from the state police academy in 1958. Over eleven years of service with the state police, I served ten years in the patrol division and was stationed at every barracks in the state. In early 1968 I was promoted to the detective division.

In early 1969 my involvement in a drug investigation with the Coventry police department resulted in an offer to become the new Coventry police chief.

Little did I realize four months after my appointment, five members of the police department were involved in a gangland style murder.

CHAPTER 2

In 1967, toward the end of my service as a state trooper, I was on a late patrol one evening out of Hope Valley barracks. Part of our patrol area covered the Town of Coventry.

A late patrol is assigned to all troopers, and we were assigned out of a particular barracks for one month. There are always two troopers. Unlike your day patrol duties where you can't go home, the late patrol trooper is allowed to go home every day and be back at the barracks by nine thirty that evening. You could drive from one end of the state of Rhode Island to the other in less than an hour. So going home every day was no big deal.

On this scheduled patrol I was partnered up with trooper Donald Miller. I worked with him once before at another barracks. He was a joy to work with, with a funny, light-hearted personality and we got along very well. If anything rattled him, I never knew it.

This particular early morning we got a call from our barracks to assist the local police in a possible threat situation. It seems this guy was waving a gun around in his side by side townhouse apartment. He was threatening to go back to a well known supper club, where he and his wife had been drinking all night.

He was accusing the owner, Mr. Harry Carlson of taking his money off the bar.

Everyone in and out of the area knew Harry Carlson, who had an impeccable reputation. The name of his establishment was the Maple Root Inn. My mother treated me to a high school graduation dinner there.

Allegedly, this drunken man was really upset, and threatened to go back to the Maple Root Inn and blow Harry up for stealing his money. The neighbors living on the other side of this duplex apartment called the Coventry police because they feared he might harm someone.

The Coventry police answered the call and two officers rolled up in a cruiser.

When we arrived, we met with the Coventry police sergeant and a special part-time policeman. They were standing at the entrance to the gravel parking lot about seventy-five feet from the front door and off to the side. It appeared to us they were attempting to hide behind the police car.

I asked "What's going on?"

The sergeant told me about the money incident and that there was a guy inside, apparently drunk.

I asked if they had tried to talk with him and who else was in the house?

They responded they had not spoken with him and had no idea who else might be in the house.

"I ain't goin' in there,' replied the special officer, 'That sum-bitch has a gun."

"Let me see what I can do," I responded.

With that, the two local police officers jumped into their police car and peeled out, never to be seen again. I looked at my partner, who stood cradling our twelve gauge shot gun. He had this wry smile on his face.

I said "Looks like it's you and me buddy".

"Yup" was all I got out of Miller.

Don was about five years junior to me so the decisions here were mine. I never doubted Miller would be there to back me up, if necessary.

We got back in our vehicle and drove up to the front door. Miller was directed to stand to the side of the door, out of sight. I told Don if this guy fired at me he was to step to the door and fire through the screen door and end this. He nodded.

Hearing the rants and complaints of this obvious drunk, I stepped to the side of the front door and knocked announcing "This is the state police". Suddenly, a little strap t-shirted older man (who reminded me of my step-father) appeared in the front door. He was about five feet tall and looked as though he had belted a few away himself. "Shorty" appeared to be about sixty or so. I recall, he had no teeth and if he would have had a corn cob pipe I would have said he was Popeye's kin. I assumed he was not my main concern.

"We have some information that there is someone here making threats against Harry Carlson and might go back to the Maple Root Inn to settle a score over some money that was allegedly stolen. Wonder if I could talk to you for a bit?"

The little man said, "Sure," pushed the door open and invited me in. I gestured to trooper Miller to stay out of sight.

I stepped into the living room and suddenly this whacko jumped around the corner of the kitchen holding a revolver. Without even flinching, he walked straight up to me and stuck a handgun in the middle of my forehead. "Yah, come on in" the dirt-bag slurred.

"Careful" I said, "that thing might go off, and if that happens, you will really piss me off".

He never lowered the gun but had a dumbfounded look on his face and said, "What?"

I suggested we go over to the kitchen table, sit down and talk about this and he could tell me what his bitch was?

There was a woman curled up on the couch in the fetal position. She was half nude wearing nothing more than a bra and a half slip. She was "out cold"; breathing, but that's about it. She was not a concern of mine either. I don't know what happened to "Shorty", but I don't remember seeing him again.

The drunk told me his name, and pointed to a seat at the table. I sat, knowing that the whole time Miller had a bead on this guy and if I went down, John Dillinger (not his name) was going too.

My host, the drunk, turned around and put his gun on the top of the refrigerator. Slurring his words he said, "Ahh, that piece of crap doesn't even have a firing pin in it".

As quickly as he said that, he wheeled around, sat and holding a larger hand gun, pointed it at me and said, "But this one does!"

Now I felt I was staring down the barrel of a fifty-five millimeter howitzer cannon. If you have ever looked down the barrel of one of those things, you would know exactly what I mean, especially, being held by some pissed off drunk.

I wondered if you could see the bullet coming and would it hurt much as it settles in between your eyes?

Calmly I asked if I could use his telephone. This was after being held as a target for about twenty minutes. There were no cell phones in those days, or portable police radios on your shoulder.

He said, "Sure, help yourself. It's on the wall right behind you".

I slowly got up from the table and took his wall phone off the hook.

At that point, he ordered me to give him my service revolver.

I looked back at him and calmly answered "The only way you, or anyone gets this gun is to take it from me. To do that, you are probably going to have to shoot me".

"Remember," I went on, "You do something stupid like that and I am really going to get pissed. You understand that?" I said, in my best stern voice.

"Oh yah," he said, "OK, you keep your gun".

I dialed headquarters and asked the night man to put the executive officer on the phone. A moment later, Hap Matthews, a newly promoted lieutenant and an assistant detective commander, came on the line.

"Yah, what's up?" Matthews asked in a groggy voice.

I just woke him. This can't be good I thought, but I needed top level advice.

"Lieutenant," I began, "I am at this house in Coventry and a man, who has been drinking, wants to go and shoot Harry Carlson. He's sitting here at his kitchen table covering me with what looks like a three fifty-seven magnum but he's allowed me to call you."

"What do you want from me," Hap Matthews asked? "Is your partner there?" I answered yes to both questions. I intimated the bad guy didn't know I had back-up.

Matthews said "It is his house, and he can do anything, short of committing murder".

"That's a possibility," I replied.

The lieutenant said "Put him to bed and get the hell out of there".

I don't know what I expected, but I didn't get much help. I knew better than argue with a superior, so I let it go, thanked the lieutenant and hung up. Inside I was growling and pissed.

After a second, I turned and stared at the drunken man, and put on my meanest look, but kept my voice calm.

"Look, this is a lot crap, so knock off your shit, put the gun away and go to bed. You also stay away from Harry Carlson and the Maple Root Inn or I'm coming back and this time it will not turn out well for you".

I turned and started toward the door leaving him standing near the refrigerator with this huge gun hanging limp by his side. I just shook my head and walked out.

Miller and I headed to our police cruiser and got in. I had to have had this frustrated look on my face and Don with his patented grin just looked at me and said,

"Want to go get a donut?"

"You crazy bastard," I yelled back at him. "I was about to get blown up by that drunken maniac, and you want to go get a donut?"

Once again Miller looked over at me and went "Yeh". We howled all the way to the donut shop.

CHAPTER 3

As a state police detective, my detective partner, Dick Sullivan and I had been investigating some drug dealings in our assigned area of the state. The state police department had no narcotics division at that time. Sullivan and I turned out to be the first narcotics investigators. We worked with local police departments assisting in obtaining information for them, assisted in drug raids, and making arrests. With the approval of headquarters and our detective commander, we always made sure the local department got credit. We were added as "giving assistance." That was fine with us.

Sullivan and I were taking the night off. I was living with a cousin, his wife and brother at the time. I had been thrown out of my own home by my wife. This occurred whenever she got the whim. She didn't need a reason.

I received a telephone call from officer Raymond King of the Coventry police department. A young, ambitious, police officer who had been on the department only a few years. I had known Ray for some time. He was in his mid twenties, dark hair, dark eyes, medium height and weight. Ray told me he had some very reliable information concerning a drug party going on in Coventry right now. Considering there was nothing his department could do about it, could I come to the station and give them some assistance? I told him I would be right there. I threw some clothes on, grabbed my plain clothes handgun and headed to the police station. It was only a little over a mile away.

I told Dolly, my cousin Ira's wife, "I might be back late so don't wait up."

"Be careful" she said.

The town solicitor (district attorney) Albert Frechette met me at the door of the police station. Frechette was a hawk-nosed little character, wearing wire-rimmed glasses, and weighing about ninety pounds. The acting police chief, and his assistant also were there, both looking confused over the situation.

Frechette said "We have a pot party going on over on Station St., just west of the town hall, and we want to raid it." For a lawyer, I was amazed at how much Frechette did not know about the law. My guess was he had never been involved in anything like this before. For that matter, neither had anyone else.

"Well goddamit, goddamit what are we going to do" bellowed Frechette?

His skinny little face was getting all red. "We just can't let this go on in our town."

Through all of this, I was wondering what Acting Chief Paul Green, and his assistant, Victor Pajak, were thinking. Pajak was popping back and forth from one foot to the other in kind of a rocking motion, scratching his rear and looking totally bewildered.

There was a big good looking man standing by and not saying anything. He stood out from the rest, was impressive in his light blue suit and tie, and carrying a light colored trench coat over his arm.

I asked Ray King, who was standing beside me, who he was? "He's the town council president Stanley Jendzejec," King replied.

He looked like he should be a leader. I walked over to the right side of the council chambers, where the president was standing, and introduced myself.

Stanley said "I know who you are. We are fully prepared to support whatever you might be able to do to help us." We shook hands and waited for the men to assemble. I decided I liked the council president.

"What can we do," Ray King asked me?

First, I told him the police could not just bust into someone's home based on information he deemed reliable, with no warrant. There certainly wasn't enough time to obtain a warrant, so we had some problems. I did have an idea, however, and properly executed, we could break up this party and make some of these kids very uncomfortable.

I suggested the acting chief bring in the patrols and get everyone together in the council chambers. I'll explain what I think we can do. Within ten minutes the council chambers had eight uniformed police officers sitting on the bench style pews. There was a total of about a dozen of us. Acting Chief Green told me the floor was mine. I rose and began unfolding my hastily assembled plan.

Based on Ray King's information, I said "You know the location of the alleged drug party. We will block off the street north and south of the house. We will put one cruiser and two men here," as I pointed to the fairly large rolling blackboard. I was drawing this up as I spoke.

"We will do the same thing on the southern side of the property. There is a small street to the rear of the house and we will station another car there. Chief Green and I will be together coordinating the activity. Lieutenant Pajak and officer King will be together and grab any stragglers that might slip through our net. Once we are all in place officer King will call the residence and, in a hurried and excited voice tell the person answering the phone to 'get the hell out of there, the cops are going to raid the place.' Then Ray will hang up immediately and simply announce over the radio to the rest of us that 'the call has been made.' My guess is we will see a bunch of pot smoking kids go flying out of the doors and with a bit of luck, right into our arms. Some of them may have marijuana and maybe other drugs in their possession and will try to throw them away. Whoever gets grabbed is to be brought back here and placed in the council chambers and guarded. We will question them for names, addresses, etc. After holding them for an hour or so, we will call their parents. This isn't going to make mom and dad too happy when they have to come and pick up their kids after midnight. Any questions? None? Good, let's go get into position."

Throughout all of this several council members sat in and observed. To my good fortune my plan worked flawlessly. We nabbed three quarters of the kids. By the way, we validated our presence at the scene because of a noise complaint in violation of a town ordinance.

No actual arrests were made. None were needed. The local press was kept in the loop throughout and they had a field day with the information and bust.

The Coventry police were gaining a new public trust and respect, something they didn't know much about in the past.

There was no reason for state police credit, so I asked Chief Green to leave that out of any press release. My detective headquarters didn't even know I had participated. I thought I might get chastised for not getting headquarters permission first. I didn't have time. It's called initiative, they taught it to me.

At the police station kids were questioned and released to upset and angry parents.

There was one young man who thought he was a real wise-guy with a bad attitude. We were in an ante room off of the council chambers.

The council president Stanley Jendzejec, the vice president Edouard Jacques, the town solicitor Al Frechette and I were all present.

I had not met any of these men formally before this night. In hindsight, I wished I had never met them.

The questioning of this young man began with Stanley asking his name.

With a crooked twist to his mouth he snarled,

"Look it up with the FBI, they have me on file."

Before he knew what was happening, I was around the corner of the small conference room table, pinned his head to the wall by his neck and stared in his face like a Marine Corps drill sergeant and forcefully said, "You don't have to like the person who is asking you the question but you sure as hell had better respect the position he holds in this community. Is that clear, or would you like to spend the night at the Hope Valley state police barracks where we can have some quiet time together to refine your attitude?" Mr. Tough Guy calmed down, apologized and cooperated.

The evening went well after that. Although no significant arrests were made, the outcome was fruitful. I got up and shook hands with everyone. I was thanked for my contribution and headed down the hallway to go home and get some sleep.

Stan Jendzejec came up beside me and thanked me again. He said he wished the Coventry police department had someone who could lead like that.

I halfheartedly replied, "Why don't you get a police chief that will give you what you want?"

Stanley said "Would you take the job?"

I couldn't believe what I had just heard. My heart jumped into my throat. All I could think of was the statement, or promise I once made: "Someday I'm going to change all of this."

I was leaving my home one afternoon in 1967, and noticed a crowd of neighbors standing around on the lawn of another neighbor who lived at the entrance of my subdivision.

My neighbor was cutting grass on his riding mower. His little three or four year old daughter was running along beside him playfully chasing the mower. He never saw her and made a turn. She slipped in the grass and her left arm went up the chute of the mower and was mangled. Most of her arm was stripped almost up to the shoulder.

When I got out of my car, the rescue squad was loading the little girl into the ambulance. She was being made ready for transport to the hospital.

Shortly thereafter a Coventry police car pulled up to begin an investigation. I knew the sergeant who was a delightful man. I graduated from high school with his son.

The murmurs in the crowd started as I stood and listened.

"Here come the Keystone Kops" I heard and "Better late than never" and on and on.

People had been doing this for years. I pretty much grew up in this town, and residents laughed at the cops then, and were still doing it.

This is when I made the statement "One day I am going to be the chief of police in this town and change all of this."

Little did I know the opportunity was about to present itself.

"Would you take the job" Stanley repeated?

I hesitated at the exit of the police station. "I don't know, I have a good job now and I don't want to ruin my life with politics."

Stan assured me there would be none of that. I could run the police department as I saw fit, and there would be no political interference. I told the town council president I would give it a good deal of thought and would get back to him.

Stanley Jendzejec said "Fine".

Shortly thereafter, I decided to use some hanging vacation time. I ran into my slinky little friend, Al Frechette, the town lawyer. Al asked me to stop by his office. Having some free time, I did.

Frechette came out of his office and asked if I could wait a few minutes and he would be right with me.

Moments later Al invited me into his office and guided me to a chair.

"Look," he began, "we in the party have been discussing you for the job as chief of police. The democratic town committee is largely in favor of you and if you agree I will push your appointment."

As I later learned the democratic town committee was made up of forty-five members. Their authority was to set policy and make suggestions to the town council. All major appointments were to be cleared through that body, before finally being enacted at an open town council meeting. I finally figured out the council meetings were largely a dog and pony show.

Proposals and any major action had already been discussed and agreed upon prior to the council meetings. Whenever there was a question from the audience the reply was usually "We will take that under advisement and report our findings at the next council meeting." That was a bunch of bull---- but that's the way it was done.

It didn't take long to find out I wasn't as popular as I thought.

A few nights later, the phone rang at my cousin's home and Dolly said it was for me. Stanley Jendzejec was on the other end asking if I could come over to the town hall and meet with the full town council. It was about nine o'clock in the evening. I went to the town hall and met with the councilmen.

Polite introductions were made all around.

Stanley started by stating the entire town council had discussed asking me to take the position as chief of police. All had agreed I was their man.

I admitted to them that I had thought about it, but as previously stated, I had a good job and didn't want to throw away more than eleven years of state police service to accept a shaky job at best. I could retire in less than nine years from the state police.

The councilmen quickly reminded me the town job would allow me to retire in fifteen years. Only six years longer wasn't bad, and I would still only be forty nine years old. Not bad, I thought.

I asked about the politics in and on the police department. Once again, I was assured there would be no interference with the operation of the police department, as long as I kept them in the loop. I had no problem with that. I hadn't suspected they were full of political crap. Color me stupid.

There was plenty of interference. It started fairly early too. It was normal for a police officer to gain advantage for himself by sucking up to a politician. This has been going on for as long as there have been cops and politicians. I simply wanted to minimize the practice.

Once again, I was told they would leave the police department to me.

I explained that I had been married and divorced once, and there was a good chance that could happen again. No one even blinked. That was not a concern of theirs. My private life was my private life.

I should have seen Eddy Jacques lurking in the background. As it turned out my appointment was not unanimous. The vote was four to one with Eddie Jacques the dissenting vote.

Had I known that, I would not have accepted their offer; they neglected to tell me.

After an hour or so of bantering back and forth, I agreed to talk with my boss, Colonel Walter Stone, Superintendant of the state police. As it turned out, taking the job was the biggest mistake of my young life.

My vacation time of a few days was over and I returned to my work as a detective. I didn't tell anyone about my offer from the Coventry town council.

I did see the colonel and we had a nice conversation. I, as did others, had a tremendous amount of respect for this man.

Colonel Stone made a comment that made it much easier to move on with my life in law enforcement.

He said, "Not everyone can be a police chief".

The superintendant then said, "If it doesn't work out you can always come back".

I couldn't believe he said that, because I never knew a trooper who left the state police and was allowed to come back, although he did take back a classmate of mine who left over some domestic issues.

The choice was clear in my mind.

I was thirty-three years old and about to become the youngest police chief in the State of Rhode Island; matter of fact, I was the youngest chief in the United States according to the National Association of Chiefs of Police.

Unfortunately I would last just over three years, and the end was not pleasant.

CHAPTER 4

In February, 1969 I was sworn in as chief of police for the town of Coventry. I would serve a six month probationary period before being given permanent tenure.

As soon as I was appointed, I began creating divisions within the police department. We instituted a detective division, (small as it might be) and a bureau of criminal identification or BCI. There were ongoing training classes with the department training officer. A public relations officer doubled as the departmental prosecution officer. He prepared court warrants, held arraignments and filed all of the necessary information into a new system. We even added a juvenile division. There had never been anything that would deal with juvenile offenders or minor offenses. Our police department was becoming totally self sustaining. In the past, the department had to rely on the state police for specialized services. It was pretty cool, when the state police detectives started coming to us for information. That was a pretty big leap from the old days. This meant we were trusted to know what we were doing.

We were rapidly becoming one of the fastest moving and expanding police departments in the state and I made certain is was easily visible. I wanted to prove my worth.

Before creating and establishing all of these new units, protocol dictated that recommendations be made to the police committee for approval.

Unquestionably there were times when misunderstandings would occur between me and the politicians over police policies. Arguing with a politician was like picking a fight with a newspaper reporter who buys his or her ink by the barrel. Dumb!

The police committee was made up of five men appointed by the town council. The committee was set up to discuss police policy and procedures. Nothing I can remember ever got approved or rejected by the committee. The council president served as police commissioner. One man on the committee owned a liquor store, and another was a professional photographer who was rumored gay. Hmmm! None of these men knew anything about law enforcement or police work, with the exception of the former police chief, Gerald A. Shippee, the man I replaced. He had been the chief for more than twenty years, but never attended a single meeting. No one seemed to care. I could understand why he didn't come, after he was forced out by the town council.

Former Chief Shippee served back in the days when political appointments were normal and acceptable. If you had a friend that was a councilman, or town committee member, you could probably get yourself appointed to the police department as a patrol officer. No training or schooling of any type was required. If you had a valid driver's license that was about all you needed. Yes, that's right, on the job training. A little scary when someone's life might depend on the decision you make.

That was all very accepted back in the day.....!

All committee members were issued these little badges that read Coventry Police Commission. As you will read later, that little badge saved Stanley Jendzejec one night, or at least he thought it did.

I was working sixteen, eighteen and even twenty hours a day. This went on for the first four months before I took a day off. I didn't dare take time off for fear I would miss something. I had my fingers in everything. What meals I had were taken in my office. My cousin's wife, Dolly, would occasionally bring me a nice home cooked meal. Financially, I couldn't afford to eat out very often.

Police departments are known to have a list of criminal charges that can be brought against those who have violated the law. The specifics of the violation are spelled out in a court warrant. The brief explanation is printed in the "violation book." The Coventry police department had none.

All charges, criminal, traffic, domestic, etc. were specifically worded and approved by the state attorney general or, on a town level, by the town solicitor.

Every state police barracks had such a book. I called the patrol commander at my last barracks, Hope Valley, and asked if I could borrow their violation book to copy the pages and I would get the book right back. He readily agreed.

I copied all the charges in the ledger most familiar to me, and most likely to be used in our department. I personally copied and typed hundreds of them on

3X5 cards and placed one copy in an indexed file in the patrol office and one in my office.

The town council allowed me to hire a secretary who quickly became my administrative assistant. Margaret McGetrick was a very capable lady. Unfortunately, I had the unpleasant task of firing her several months later. I fabricated a story that she inadvertently leaked some confidential information that came out of my office.

All these years, I have imagined what poor Margaret has been thinking. Why was I being replaced? Why am I getting fired? Truth is, she never did anything wrong. I was learning the art of politics quickly. She was a victim of a political father wanting her position for a friend and neighbor and Margaret had to go. She got another job with the school department, but didn't seem to hold her firing against me. She was very gracious. Her husband? Not so much.

My next assistant was as close to perfect as anyone could get. She was better than good. Mrs. Alice Brouillard had been a secretary to high ranking military officers in Europe. I shared much with her, and trusted her with my life. Mrs. "B" was very professional, pleasant and extremely intelligent. Mrs. "B" remained with the police department after I left and I could almost guarantee she held the place together until another chief was found to replace me. She was an absolute asset to the department.

Even the citizens, who couldn't have cared less in the past, were beginning to chant the praises of their police department. I drew up protection programs for more remote areas of our town and increased patrol power and visibility in isolated areas. Residents who rarely ever saw a local police cruiser, began to see them regularly now. I still give credit for all of this to the cooperation of the department members.

The men worked hard and were dedicated to making the Coventry police department the best it could be. No, we didn't increase manpower, we simply used every resource we had, and the men were doing multiple tasks. No one was complaining.

In the first six months we cut criminal activity down by seventy-five percent. Traffic citations and prosecutions were up one hundred percent. Town roads were no longer race tracks. There were no fixes. Everybody paid the fiddler. After a time, though, I will admit, I had to step in and alter some of the court summonses. Every pending court summons had to cross my desk with a copy of the motor vehicle operators driving record. For example, if a person had been operating a vehicle for thirty-five years or so and had never had a traffic violation and the alleged violation was forty miles per hour in a twenty-five mile per hour zone I would pull that violation ticket. With knowledge of the issuing officer, and with his blessing, we would turn that court ticket into a warning. The offender did not have to appear in court and nothing would affect the operator's license. Finally, our secretary would write the offender a brief letter on department stationary explaining what had been done. The letter was signed by me and the issuing officer.

What a positive impact that had on public opinion and on the officers themselves! It was amazing what positive things we accomplished in the first few months, and then, a couple of months later, "The Bomb Went Off"!

CHAPTER 5

During my reformation of the police department, I bought a small, two story, two bedroom cottage in town. This little place was right next to the railroad tracks and used to be the servants quarters for a much larger farm. The farm ceased operation years ago and the land was sold off in smaller parcels.

A local freight train came through twice a day. Everything in the house shook. I think the term "shake, rattle & roll" was coined in honor of this little dump. When I was married I had a very nice home in a middle class neighborhood and now I had this little shack, but it was my little shack. I loved it. It was mine and mine alone.

Somehow I learned Officer Tom Jones had lost his place to live. I invited him to move in with me until he got his feet back on the ground. Rent was reasonable; free. I had an extra room so what did it matter? Tom agreed but protested the rental rate. He wanted to pay something. Again, I told him it was not necessary.

Every once in awhile Jones would sneak up to my bank and deposit some money in my account. Took me a few months to figure out how I got this extra money in my checking account.

Tom was about six feet tall, one hundred and sixty pounds and was pretty squared away. He was a single guy and didn't seem to have much luck with the ladies. On the other hand, he might have expected too much. I should have learned from him, I guess. I believe we became known as the odd couple. It wasn't malicious, the guys at the department were just fooling around.

One day very shortly after I was appointed chief, I stopped at an old gas station and Tom was working there. We talked for a bit and I asked why he didn't pursue a career as a police officer?

He said, "Ah, I don't know, I've thought about it but can't seem to bring myself to apply." I probably wouldn't get picked." I told him I might be able to help with that.

Shortly, thereafter Tom became a Coventry police officer. The appointment was a good move on my part.

CHAPTER 6

One very unfortunate responsibility many state police barracks commanders had, as did headquarters, was to charge motorists whether it was a good charge or a questionable one. I was involved in one dandy I'll never forget. I vowed never to let this happen on my police department.

I was stationed at Hope Valley state police barracks near the Connecticut state line. One evening, it was bitterly cold with rain freezing instantly on the highway. A car, driven by an older Jewish man, with his wife and daughter as passengers, was travelling northbound on the highway. He was headed down a small hill and came into a corner, slid down an embankment and into the woods and struck some trees. Everyone in the car was hurt to some degree, but the wife was the worst. She was about sixty years old and got bounced around violently in the front seat. As it turned out, she had a broken leg and some pretty nasty cuts on her head and face.

I was dispatched to the scene, and was there moments after the crash. There was no one around, and the family was not even out of the car yet. I assisted the man out of the car, and after a brief check, he indicated he wasn't badly hurt. As mentioned, the wife had a broken leg. I turned immediately to the daughter to check her injuries. I called for the rescue squad, such as it was in

Hope Valley. It took them about half an hour to get to the scene. Not their fault, the roads were treacherous.

The young girl was in obvious pain and had quite a gash in her head. I spoke to her calmly and told her I was going to help her, but, I was going to need her to be brave. She whimpered she would try.

We had no splints and very limited medical supplies in the police cruiser. I needed a splint and some bandages. His car trunk had popped open and I saw a hammer lying on the floor. I grabbed the hammer and found a towel in the rear seat. I returned to the mother, who by now was being cradled by her crying and apologetic husband. I was successful in removing her foot from underneath the dash. A splint was fashioned from the hammer handle, using the towel as a binder.

She was more than brave, she never made a sound or complained about anything and I knew I must be causing her pain. The rescue unit finally arrived, got her stabilized and took her off to the hospital which was about twenty miles to the southwest.

The father and daughter accompanied the mother to the hospital in the rescue wagon. I returned to the barracks after drawing a diagram of the accident scene and gathering the information I needed to complete the report.

When I got back to the state police barracks, my lieutenant said, "What did the scene look like?"

I told the lieutenant the roads were glare ice and I barely made it to the scene myself and I had chains on my tires.

The accident happened on a very severe curve that was temporary, due to road construction. I did not feel there was adequate warning approaching that curve; no blinking lights, signs, etc. The driver just lost control and went down the embankment. There was no indication of speed or reckless driving.

The lieutenant told me to make out a warrant and charge him with going too fast for existing road conditions.

"What?" I blurted out. "You want me to charge him?"

"Yes," replied my patrol commander.

"But . . . ," I stammered.

" Just keep your mouth shut and do what you're told Simmons."

Wow, I thought, and just walked out of the patrol commander's office. There was no way I wanted to charge this man with anything.

I did not make the rules, my superiors did. I really liked my lieutenant, but I lost a great deal of admiration and respect for him that night. I will never forget my patrol commander's remark as he demanded I charge the motorist.

"Fu#@ um, charge um," he said. "Let them foot the cost of defending a lawsuit. We get represented for free by the state". My gut was rumbling. I was getting mad and that wasn't going to do me any good at all.

The older Jewish gentleman was arraigned in Third District court in Westerly, Rhode Island. The man pleaded not guilty and a trial date was set for two weeks.

What kind of a crumby bastard did this man think I was? I couldn't very well go to him and tell him I was just following orders. I felt I would have only insulted his intelligence. Worse yet, I learned he was on his way to Washington, DC to accept a government job but because he was held in Rhode Island for two weeks awaiting trial he missed his opportunity. He had, by the way, quit his present job and now had nothing. I also came to learn that he was a Jewish immigrant. For most of his pre-adult life he was confined to a German concentration camp and had the serial numbers tattooed on his forearm to prove it. He watched as his father, mother, uncles and aunts were burned in the ovens.

On the witness stand I told the truth about the accident and how it happened. After the trial was over the Jewish man walked over to me and thanked me for telling the truth. He knew I was purposely blowing the state's case. He went on to thank me for the kind caring treatment I rendered at the accident scene. I felt like a real scum ball. He said he knew I had testified to the truth and that is why the judge returned a not guilty verdict. His parting remarks to me were he had received better treatment in the concentration camp. If there were a hole large enough I would have jumped into it and pulled the dirt over me.

I was in Judge Trumpetto's chambers after the court session was over as was the state attorney general's assistant, Vincent Cianci. Some of you might remember him as the former mayor of Providence, Rhode Island, who did time in prison for beating up his wife's boyfriend. As I recall, there were other charges brought against him and he is now a convicted felon. Other than being a real asshole, he is now a local folk hero who got re-elected as mayor of Providence. He now hosts a television talk show in Providence. He is a latter day "Blago".

While we were in the judge's office, Cianci turned to me and began to chew me out in earnest because I told the truth on the witness stand.

"You know that stupid answer you gave about road conditions being severe?"

I answered, "I remember".

Cianci ranted on, "Well, you dumb-ass, you blew the case for us."

I replied with, "So you wanted me to lie on the witness stand, is that right?"

"Goddamned right I did, you asshole," Cianci raved.

"Do you know what you did to my conviction rate?"

The judge was just sitting there taking all of this in without offering a word to stop this lunatic. I figured I might be able to get a shot in and the judge would let it pass, also. So I looked at Vinny Cianci and asked if he would like to go outside for a moment?

"Why the hell should I go outside with you?"

"Because I am about to shove your head up your ass, and I don't want to do it in front of the judge." I walked out leaving him sputtering and spitting on himself.

Needless to say, that wasn't the last of it. When I got back to the barracks, the lieutenant was waiting. I was directed into the patrol commander's office and the ass-chewing began. "Do you know what you did in court?"

"Yes," I replied, "I didn't lie on the witness stand like Cianci wanted me to". The lieutenant then advised me I was in big shit, and would probably lose some time off for my actions. Considering we lived at the state police barracks, and worked a sixteen hour day, loss of time off for a state trooper is about the worst punishment you could get other than being brought up on charges and fired. I was mentally preparing for the inevitable.

For a time, I caught numerous dirty assignments, or as we called them, shit details. I was working nights for weeks, which meant I also had to stay at the barracks days because I wasn't allowed to go home. I would be assigned all night desk duty, and wound up washing and cleaning all eight cruisers at three o'clock in the morning. I washed, scrubbed and waxed vinyl floors in the barracks. I knew this was all part of the game and pretty much blew it off. Some state police patrol commanders could be real beauties (bastards) when they felt like it. Others were excellent to work for. The more time on the job, the less crap you had to put up with. Regardless, the state police were, and are, one of the finest organizations in the country, law enforcement or otherwise.

This story is only one of many that reinforced why I felt as I did. I would not let those things happen when I was the chief of police.

I had an idea about cut and dried investigations. Kind of like "screw um, charge um". A decision was made to reinvestigate more serious and complicated crimes.

OfficerTom Jones was turning out to be relentless as an investigator. That wasn't even his job. He pursued this on his own time. On occasion I would ask him to re-investigate a complaint that our detectives were preparing for prosecution.

One such incident was when our detectives arrested and charged an individual with passing worthless checks. The charges and warrants had been drawn.

Just before the court arraignment Tom came into my office and said, "Chief, you know the guy that is charged with passing bad checks?"

"Yes, I remember".

"He didn't do it".

I just looked at him and told him, "Go on, convince me".

"I found the guy who did pass the worthless checks and he admitted it. We are charging the wrong guy." Tom then produced a signed confession.

I got up from my desk and walked over to Tom, shook his hand and said, "Nice job".

I then contacted the detectives and told them to release their suspect based on new information, and count that as a lesson learned. This action was repeated several times over the course of my relationship with Tom Jones.

"That's what you call good police work".

CHAPTER 7

On another occasion, I received a complaint from a local business owner who was a friend and former school-mate. For department members, this was to be another lesson learned.

This gentleman owned a local ice cream creamery. He told me his complaint really wasn't a big deal, but some of my police officers would stop at his kitchen in the early morning hours and bring ice cream back to the police station for the other guys on the night shift. Of course, no one ever paid for anything, or even offered. Apparently, my police officers just walked in and grabbed what they wanted and walked out.

This occurred shortly after I was appointed and before the murder turned the department upside down. One of the officers was a probationary officer, and didn't think he was doing anything wrong by helping himself to ice cream and other goodies. He was doing as ordered by the night sergeant, and was just getting treats for the other guys. He simply figured he had to do what he was told by a superior. Oddly enough, this was much the same as an athletic contest where a player gets away with throwing the first punch, but the one who retaliates gets nailed. Such was the case here.

It was obvious I had to do something to stop this immediately, so I called the police officer to my office, and confronted him with what I knew. He admitted he had taken some ice cream and offered to go pay the businessman for his pilfering. I told him it was too late for that. You are going to get a letter of reprimand in your service record and you will be assigned one hundred hours of extra duty. I asked the officer, Dennis Perry, if he knew he had committed theft.

He said he never thought of it that way, and apologized. I went on to tell him I knew he could appeal any punishment I would give him to his union, if he chose, but I would counsel against it.

"Your union might file suit against the department. I would probably lose, and have to rescind the punishment, at which point I would flat out fire you and put you up on charges."

Perry looked beaten, "I'll accept any punishment chief," and with that I dismissed him.

Command isn't fun. I felt terrible about having to discipline him, but I couldn't let him know that.

In actuality, the officer served thirty four hours of his punishment. I dismissed the rest of the hours because of his good attitude and no complaints.

The word was out that the good old days of graft and pilfering were over.

Tragically, this was the same officer activated by the National Guard during the Viet Nam war and went away for nearly a year. When he came home he had a brand new baby . . . . only it wasn't his. We didn't have a department chaplain yet so I counseled him and his wife for hours. Eventually we seemed to work things out and they stayed together.

This was also the same police officer who was told to stand guard at the entrance to the sand bank where the murder was committed. He was eventually acquitted in court of being an accomplice, but, by then he had been fired and had no job. The last I heard he was driving a school bus. This poor man had a lot of luck. . . . except it appeared it was mostly bad. In truth, he was really a nice guy and I liked him. His was just another life ruined over the murder; something he had nothing to do with. Talk about stinking circumstances.

CHAPTER 8

Three months after my appointment, in May 1969, Stan Jendzejec called me at 3:00 AM and told me we had the son of a town committee member locked up and my policemen were going to arraign him in a few hours. Stanley suggested I call the station and have the young man released. I asked Stanley if he knew what the man had done. Stanley told me it was just a little misunderstanding, nothing serious. I took him at his word, called the station and spoke with Sergeant Al Lameroux and told him to release the boy. We know where he lives in the town and can get him back anytime.

I walked into the station at about 8:00 AM that morning to prepare for a parade in the City of East Providence. My men and women had been invited to march in that parade.

The night sergeant approached me with this disgruntled look on his face and said, "I thought things were going to be different around here with you as chief?"

"What do you mean by that," I asked?

"Well, chief, you told all of the men that you would back them. What the hell kind of backing do you call it when a drunken punk takes a couple of punches at a police officer in Joe's Diner before a hundred people, and swears his head off at them? It took three of us to get him out of there."

"Added to that," the sergeant went on, "There were two other guys with him, how come they didn't get released?"

After hearing this, I flew to the telephone and called Stanley Jendzejec back. I got him out of bed. "Stan," I said, "I need for you to get a hold of Eddie Rekas and have his son back at the police station in thirty minutes or I will have someone from the department pick you up and charge you with interfering with the duties of a police officer." I was livid.

Stan replied "I will call his father and see what he wants to do".

"I don't give a goddamn what Rekas wants to do, you just get his kid back in here, and Stanley, I am dead serious."

The troublemaker appeared within a half hour, and was carted away with his other two companions. This certainly did not make me the most popular person in Eddie Rekas' life and, of course, the democratic town committee where Rekas was a member.

Rekas came into my office for a talk and, told his son's side of the story, all the while making the boy look like the victim. The elder Rekas was questioning my judgment. I told him he should probably let little Eddie Jr. grow up and accept responsibility for his choices. I added that his comments were a little unfounded since we had statements from at least a dozen patrons who watched his son make a fool of himself.

This was pretty much the beginning of the "Big Dig" meaning the hole I was digging for myself. Challenging a town committee member wasn't one of the smartest things I had done. There may have been another way to handle the situation.

All I was trying to do was establish the credibility of the police department, and one way or another, I was going to do it.

So that you know, Eddie Jr. pleaded not guilty and a couple of weeks later the district court judge threw the case out for lack of evidence.

Truth is Frechette who was still the town lawyer, talked with the judge and had a little something to do with the case getting tossed. Imagine that?

CHAPTER 9

Good, bad or indifferent, police work was my life.

I was happy as the chief of police. I didn't want anything for myself personally. I enjoyed watching the department grow and was very proud of the men that heeded my direction. They used to be the literal laughing stock of Keystone Kops that became an efficient, specialized law enforcement agency. I don't remember reaping the harvest, or getting any kind of tangible reward, except for my salary. By the way, I made more money as a state police detective. I watched as plans I had hatched turn into actual true to life working programs that produced results.

The community was well protected.

We climbed back from the depths of anguish and embarrassment after a long year of suffering from the disastrous effects of the murder. I had some bumper stickers made that simply said "Support YOUR Local Police Department." Every time I was invited to speak to a civic group, I would make it a point to stress we were the citizen's police department. "We are your police officers," I would tell them. Respect was coming, and we were gaining supporters, by leaps and bounds.

There was a tremendous reward when I personally worked with youth groups. Some of them were heading in the wrong direction. Taking a path that would eventually lead them to regret the choices of their youth.

Let me tell you right here about what I had heard for years about juveniles and arrest records.

Everyone has heard the fairy tale that if a youth is arrested for a crime, even a minor one, there will be no police record after that person turns eighteen.

I am here to tell you that is baloney. Before computers, all police departments would maintain a card index file stating the person's name and address and a mini-description of the crime that was committed. This card usually referred to a larger paper arrest sheet. The story is once a person becomes of legal adult age these records will be destroyed and the individual begins life anew. Once again, "baloney." There will be an arrest record somewhere in that department forever regardless of court orders to expunge, or anything else. Those records can come back to haunt you, especially in today's society with computers. Best antidote? Don't commit a crime.

Even as a state trooper, I was aware of the teen-age problem at a local Dairy Queen. There was a gang of unruly teenagers who hung out at this location. Their ring leader was a young man named Eddie Hoxie. Coventry had its own "Fonzie." Remember him?

Customers complained about being harassed by the kids and the establishment was losing business. The owners of the Dairy Queen would call the Coventry police, but little or nothing was done. In fact, it got to the point that the Dairy Queen owners had to hire a police officer to keep the peace.

One night the kids got together and jumped the untrained special, or part-time, police officer, chased him out into the highway and even pulled his pants down, hooting and yelling and chasing him down the road. The officer finally got back to the lot, jumped into his car and went home never to be seen again.

Shortly after I became chief of police I was made aware that complaints were still coming in about the Dairy Queen. The kids complained there was no place to hang out and nothing to do. I decided to meet with them and listen first hand to their gripes. I got a business owner to donate the use of his banquet room in a local restaurant and we did hold a meeting.

Hoxie was about seventeen years old when I met him for the first time at the meeting. I would think that was a memorable meeting for Hoxie. He was mouthing off and trying to incite a group of about twenty five kids. As I recall, I walked over and confronted him. He had this smart-ass smirk on his face. Without warning, I gave him a quick little shot in the mouth. I thought that might help straighten Hoxie out. I was wrong.

Before I could get anything going, Hoxie gathered up his group of wise guys and continued to harass the patrons at the Dairy Queen.

One night they were all assembled in the parking lot. The owners called and said they were raising hell. A plan was forming in my mind so I called the town highway superintendent, Tom Kenahan. His brother and I were state troopers together, and started a hot rod club with some local boys, several years back.

I asked Tom if he had access to a school bus since they were all parked at the town garage. He said he did. I told Tom what I had in mind and wondered if we could borrow a bus and driver. Tom answered he would drive the bus himself and said he would be there in ten minutes.

Within thirty minutes, I had every police officer we had, plus some minor assistance from the state police, in the Dairy Queen parking lot. We herded the kids into a corner, and here comes Tom Kenahan with the school bus. Hoxie was giving his friends lessons on how to direct traffic as he stood in the middle of the highway. We loaded all of the kids into the bus. Abruptly, the kids stopped mouthing off and became very quiet, obviously not knowing what the hell was going on. We took the kids back to the police station and into the council chambers. That room was getting some pretty good use.

My officers got names and addresses, and then they were told they would be charged with criminal trespass, loitering, disturbing the peace and whatever else I could think of. I told them they would all have criminal records and that would really screw up their lives.

During all of this Hoxie remained defiant still out in the roadway.

I walked out to him, leaned over and whispered in his ear, "How about you and I go back to the station and have a little chat, just the two of us?" I did this while I was standing with my full 185 pound weight on Hoxie's foot and grinding just a bit.

I heard Hoxie answer with this pained look and weak voice, "No sir".

"Good," I said, "Get on the bus".

The rest of the kids were held until about midnight and then we started calling their parents to come and pick them up. Once again, there were a lot of unhappy moms and dads.

Hoxie had been arrested a dozen times, and I informed him we would harass him for the rest of his miserable life. Subsequently, Eddie Hoxie ended up joining the Marine Corps. Boom, he was gone. Aha, I thought they will straighten his little smart ass out at Parris Island. Been there, done that.

Wrong again. Hoxie was out within a month on a general discharge. I never knew how he did that or what he did to get out of the marines. Maybe the Marine Corps is letting up a little and going soft and has stopped babysitting America's screwed up civilians. I still get a kick out of the "Old Corps" description of USMC equals Uncle Sam's Misguided Children. Hoxie fit that description perfectly.

I always likened the U. S. Marines to the Rhode Island State Police. They both instilled a pride that lasts a lifetime. All ex-marines will know what I am talking about.

After I was fired, I was in a local establishment one evening and here comes Eddie Hoxie. I did not expect to see Hoxie's hand shoot out and grab mine.

"Chief Simmons, you really got screwed." He went on to say, "Who the hell do we follow now? You were our leader. I know we gave you some bad times but there ain't one guy who doesn't feel down deep that you are one hell of a man. You kept us from getting into serious trouble and watched over us when we needed watching. I saw a lot of guys get spaced out on drugs or get busted for stealing or something real bad but you were always there climbing up our asses. You never hurt anybody. You are OK in our book and if there is ever a time we can do anything for you, just yell."

Quite a speech coming from Ed Hoxie. I was more than mildly impressed. I saw Eddie Hoxie around town for years after that and each time he made it a point of smiling and yelling encouragement. One never knows.

CHAPTER 10

There were long hours and constant activity but there was also time for some comic relief.

I remember the night clearly. It was just after 6:00 PM on July 3rd. I had just finished a brief evening meal and was headed back to my office. Hang on, that needs a bit more explanation.

The police department is housed in the town hall which was a long, one story colonial brick building. All of the town offices were spread throughout the structure as well as a couple of departments in the basement level. The lower level also housed two jail cells. Not the type you most commonly see in the movies or on TV. Actually the cells were constructed with metal slats from top to bottom. Looked something like Grandma's pie crust. These cells were installed in a large concrete room.

Sounds carried easily, and in many cases, voices echoed off of the walls and down the hallways. This is where the fun began.

My appointment as chief of police was five months earlier. This particular early evening was really nice and warm. I was thirty four years old and the youngest police chief in the state. I was dressed in a short sleeved open neck shirt and a regular pair of slacks. I didn't have a uniform yet and probably wouldn't have worn it if I did have one. One bad habit I had was not carrying a gun. Many occasions, while a state police detective, I would go out on an investigation and my pistol would be back at the barracks detective's room in the drawer of my desk. I must have been lucky though, because I never got into a gun fight, so why did I need a gun. I don't like guns.

Many years ago, a state trooper once related to me that he never carried a blackjack. I asked, "Why"?

He held his hands up and said, "If you can't take them with these I would just pull my gun out and shoot their asses".

I was impressed. He was nuts as were many troopers I worked with, but their stories are better left for another time.

For one reason or another, or probably for no reason at all, I was wearing a snub-nose thirty eight caliber Smith & Wesson. I had a small holster on my left hip. Not one of the dizzy looking, uncomfortable strap holster things we see the "real" TV cops wearing.

I was trying to quit smoking cigarettes and switched to those small Tiparillo cigars, thinking they were better for you. I had a box of those little cigars in my top pocket and a lit one in my mouth. I liked to chew on the plastic mouthpiece.

Entering the town hall from the west side of the building, you came instantly into a hallway. Directly across the hall was the entrance to the patrol office for the police department. Before going down the hallway, there was a door that led down a flight of stairs to the basement level, the cell block and my office.

At the far end of the basement level, the officers got together and, on their time off, they built me a nice office, with a smaller ante room office for my new administrative assistant. I really appreciated their efforts.

As I walked into the patrol office I heard such yelling, screaming and swearing I couldn't believe it. I walked up to the desk sergeant and asked what all the noise was about?

Sergeant Ernie Tellier said, "Oh, that's just Marcel the town drunk. Every now and then he ties one on and we have to bring him in and dry him out. Then we send him home".

I said "Sarge, there is a council meeting going on in chambers and he has to be disturbing everyone".

Sergeant Tellier responded with "There isn't much we can do."

About that time one of my special police officers walked in. I had gone to school with Doug Moriarty and we had been friends for years.

We really didn't speak, because I spun around and brushed past Doug and said, "Well, I'll shut him up".

I bolted down the stairs, flung open the door to the cell block and went in. There was the noise machine spewing out his opinions on everything from women's voting rights to Barbie's breast size. Man, this guy could have taught profanity classes to the truck drivers, drunken sailors and Marine DI's.

Marcel fashioned himself as a Dapper Dan, about forty two years old, and he thought he looked like Clark Gable. Damned if he didn't, with his pencil mustache, the wavy dark hair combed straight back and his short sleeved sport shirt open halfway to the waist.

He was sitting on the metal cot just wailing away.

I walked up to the cage and yelled, **"HEY"**.

He looked up and yelled back, "Who the hell are you?" followed by a stream of profanity.

"I am the chief of police and if you don't stop the yelling and calm down you are going to regret it".

His reply (at the top of his lungs) was, "Get the hell out of here, you asshole" and then more profanity.

In my top pocket along with the Tiparillos were two cherry bombs that had come into my possession. Some of my guys had confiscated them from some kids carrying them for the fourth of July.

I still had a Tiparillo burning in my fingers.

Glaring back at Marcel, I said, "I'm giving you one last warning to shut your mouth and calm down or you are going to suffer some consequences you aren't going to expect".

"Get the hell out of here" and more profanity was the response.

"OK, but don't say I didn't warn you."

I turned my back on Marcel and made it appear I was walking out. He was still screaming. I reached in my top shirt pocket and pulled out a cherry bomb, bent down slightly and lit it. I flung it down to the far end of the cell. Marcel couldn't have seen what I was doing.

I spun around, yanked my snub nosed revolver out of its holster, pointed it directly at Marcel and said loudly "OK Jerk, you asked for it". At that instant the cherry bomb went off. There was a thunderous explosion in this concrete enclosure. I know my ears were ringing for a bit.

Smoke everywhere. Looking through the smoke I noticed Marcel had jumped up on his metal cot, pulled his knees up to his chest, and was whiter than the whitest sheet I had ever seen. He didn't say a word.

Without acknowledging him at all, I pulled the gun back, looked at the barrel and then back at Marcel and said, to no one in particular, "How the hell did I miss at that range"? I won't miss this time".

Marcel looked at me with the widest eyes I had ever seen and whispered, "I won't make a sound," and hunkered down trying to make himself invisible.

I looked at the pitiful sight of this drunk and said, "Alright, but don't ever let me see you back in this police station again, do you understand?" He just shook his head yes. I noticed as he crouched on the cot, the inside part of his right leg was soaked.

Walking out of the cellblock, I saw Sgt. Tellier and Officer Doug Moriarty streaking down the stairs, gawking at me as I slid my gun back in my holster.

Before they could say anything I said, "He won't bother us anymore".

Sgt. Tellier, a 30 year veteran looked at Officer Moriarty and said, "Shit, the chief just shot Marcel. What the hell are we going to do with the body?" I walked away to the far end of the building and into my office.

Sgt. Tellier told me later they had to pry Marcel's hands loose from the bunk and the bars to get him out of the cell.

A few weeks later, I had a golf date with a friend who was a manager at a local diner. He also took care of the bar. I recall walking into the bar to ask my friend what time we were scheduled to tee off. Out of the corner of my eye, I noticed a guy with a little pencil mustache got off a bar stool and furtively headed to an exit at the other end of the room. I really didn't get a good look at him so a questioned my friend, Buzz, "Who was that"?

"Marcel," Buzz replied.

"What was he drinking," I asked?

"Soda water," Buzz said.

"Oh".

PART TWO

CHAPTER 11

I still recall vividly standing in an ornate New England courtroom in April 1972, before a superior court Judge. I raised my right hand and stated my name: "Harvey Curtis Simmons," I uttered. I heard myself saying the words, but didn't recognize that it was me saying them.

The courthouse was as old and retiring, as an old New England building ought to be. A full set of wide stone steps led to the large double front doors. Once in the building, you ascended a few more wooden steps, turned right and into the superior courtroom. The main floor accommodated viewers as did the semi-circular upper level gallery. The galleries housed several attorneys, and their clients, just waiting their turn to go before Judge Anthony Giannini. The judge was a pleasant looking, middle aged Italian man and was considerably younger than most superior court judges. I had met Judge Giannini on occasion, but did not really know him.

As I stepped before the bench with my lawyer at my side, the judge nodded in almost a friendly manner and gave the indication he was sorry for what he was about to say, but made it clear, he had a job to do.

Strangely enough, the night before this hearing, my brother called me.

He said, "Congratulations, you're going back to work". I couldn't believe my ears.

Moreover, I wanted to know where my brother, Don, got his information. He told me one of the passengers in his car-pooling crowd was married to Judge Giannini's secretary. She typed Judge Giannini's order to dismiss any and all charges against me, and return me to work as the chief of police, with all back pay and privileges. I could not believe what I was hearing! After months and months of waiting, anticipating and unemployment I was going to have my day. Maybe life was fair after all. I didn't go out, I didn't feel like celebrating, I didn't call anyone, I just went to bed.

In the morning, I awoke, showered, put on a suit and prepared to meet my attorney, Felix Appolonia, at his office. We drove to the courthouse together, where I found myself standing before Judge Giannini. My heart was pounding as the court clerk, Thomas Moody, started to read an indictment charging me with extortion, by way of threatening to expose Stanley M. Jendzejec to disgrace and injure his reputation, with intent to compel Jendzejec to resign, against his will, as president and member of the Coventry Town Council. I heard the words clearly as stated by Clerk Moody. They bounced off my ears like someone was hammering a nearby bass drum. After my telephone conversation with my brother, this couldn't be happening. This was a nightmare.

I stood there thinking that the injurious charge was totally bogus. Two local newspapers reported that Stanley had been contemplating resigning his positions for 6 months. Eddie Jacques reported in the press that all of the councilmen knew for six months prior that Stanley Jendzejec was going to resign. So, where did the attorney general come up with the basis for that charge?

Later, through a friend, I was to learn what happened. More detail will come later, but briefly, the states attorneys general learned I was to be dismissed with no charges. The attorney general, Richard Isreal, called Judge Giannini and told him he had better not return me to my position as chief of police, because he was going to indict me. The indictment would put the judge in a very bad political position, considering the judge was a political appointee. Plus, Isreal was going to run for Governor, and he, Giannini, might want to count him as a friend. In other words, don't get on his bad side. Obviously, late that night, or early the following morning, Judge Giannini changed his position, and an indictment was issued.

No big deal! I was only facing 15 years in prison, a $15,000 fine and/or both!

My new attorney, John Tramonti, was a top-notch criminal attorney and recommended by a very close friend who had some dealings with him in the past. My first lawyer, Attorney Appolonia, knew he was in way over his head, and to his credit, he backed away and deferred to Atty. Tramonti of Providence. This turned out to be an excellent move, for once.

Dan Shea, a superior court clerk, was in the courtroom to record the proceedings when a grand jury was convened. This was in a different courtroom from the one I was charged in. Dan was a man in his mid sixties, tall, thin, light skinned and very Irish. I had known Dan from being in and out of the courthouse many times over the years in my state police duties.

Dan knew people were being selected for a secret grand jury. "Secret" means the "subject" of the investigation is not supposed to know what is happening until after he, or she, is indicted. Like the lamb being led to the slaughter. Try keeping that quiet in a small New England town. Try keeping that secret anywhere.

My telephone rang, and on the other end was a friend informing me of the secret grand jury. I called Felix immediately.

Felix said, "I will call the attorney general right now and arrange a meeting". He called back a while later, and told me we were going to Providence.

We were ushered into the attorney general's office. Attorney General Isreal appeared to be totally disinterested in what we had to say until I told him I learned that I had the right to testify before the grand jury, and I wanted to exercise that right.

The following day I was invited to testify. Had they not invited me, they would have violated my rights all over the place and Isreal knew it.

I was lead into the jury room by Clerk Shea and, was directed to a single chair in the middle of the courtroom facing the grand jury. Talk about feeling isolated and alone.

I knew the attorney general's assistant, Bob DeCosta, was leading the grand jury. Testimony is submitted only by the prosecutor. The person being charged has no representation, and usually the jury makes up its own mind. In this case, I was there to break up their party.

After I was seated, I introduced myself to the men and women in the jury box. None of their faces were familiar, with the exception of one member. He was an outstanding former halfback for the neighboring high school.

My statement began with, "I don't know any of you personally except Mr. Andy Gough. We played football against each other".

My speech was very slow, and deliberate, as I continued, "At no time have I ever intentionally, or unintentionally, done anything that would bring embarrassment or disgrace upon my town. Everything I have done has been with the best intentions and always to create a safer environment for our community. Rumors of all sorts will abound about me, and certainly, there have been those people that do not like me. I understand that, but in the end I get along very well with myself. I am not ashamed nor do I have anything to hide. I sincerely hope you will take my comments into consideration when deliberating my fate. Thank you for your time and kind consideration".

There are many instances when the prosecutor hammers away with all kinds of unsupported and circumstantial evidence. Mr. DeCosta, who I also knew from my state police days, tried three times to get me indicted and failed. The jury just wasn't buying his tales of alleged corruption, mismanagement of police department affairs and other minimal concerns of little or no consequence.

As an example, our police department had a copy machine and we charged 50 cents a copy for accident reports and other records desired by proper authorities. My executive officer put that money in a cash box and we bought flowers for special occasions for department members' families, cards for sick family members or the officers themselves and other small incidentals. To my knowledge, no one ever touched any of that money for personal use. I don't believe there was ever over $50 in the box at one time. A slip for expenditures was always in the box. Yet, when they charged me with misappropriation of funds; those were the funds they referred to.

DeCosta reported his findings to AG Isreal, and after three frustrating tries, the attorney general himself announced he would come before the grand jury in person. According to witnesses, Isreal, a wiry little balding, hawk-nosed lawyer, stepped before the grand jury and after bashing me some more he told them he would keep them there for however long it took to get an indictment. They finally gave in.

Atty. Tramonti stood to my left and a sheriff to my right. I saw familiar faces in the courtroom. They must have thought I had myself under control. I showed no emotion. No one knew of my brother's phone call.

Clerk Moody asked "To this charge how do you plead?" I was too numb to say anything. My attorney broke the silence with "Not guilty," your honor. The sound of his voice brought me back to reality.

The attorney general's assistant rose to make a recommendation to Judge Giannini that his department had no objection to personal recognizance.

Judge Giannini said, "Fine, Mr. Simmons you are placed on one thousand dollars personal recognizance."

The judge lightly pounded his gavel and stepped off the bench. He court clerk took my oath, as I assured him I would appear at the appointed time ready for trial.

I walked out of the courthouse with my two attorneys. Attorney Tramonti would represent me at my criminal trial, and attorney Appolonia would handle my civil procedure concerning my firing as a town official. What a day, and it wasn't over!

Upon leaving the courthouse, Attorney Tramonti made it very clear I was to speak with no one. No interviews, no reporters, no press releases. There will be no remarks, counter charges or anything from our side. I got the message, I was to keep my mouth shut or he would not represent me. John was willing to handle my case but it had to be on his terms.

He added, "By the way, I will require a Five Hundred Dollar retainer. If I can't help you, I will tell you. You will have to do what I say, and play by my rules."

I nodded in agreement. Now, where am I going to come up with $500? I knew if I opened my mouth I would vomit.

* * *

Regarding my civil attorney, Felix Appolonia, and his attack on the charge of insubordination. We were beaten in Superior court and Felix knew it. It didn't help any that Judge Giannini was Appolonia's law school classmate. I guess it shouldn't have. Honest justice is honest justice. Want to buy a bridge over some swamp land in Arizona?

Recall the telephone call I got from my brother, concerning the superior court judge's decision to put me back to work with all back pay and allowances? I was really fired on a charge of insubordination. There were never any criminal charges filed against me. Anyway, we need to go in another direction to this sordid tale. I'll bring you back to the superior court trial, but first, you need to know the circumstances of the insubordination

Allegedly, because of an altercation with George Carter, an ex-Pawtucket, Rhode Island cop, I was told by the town council not to return to work until approved to do so by the council. It's a long and involved story, but the council said there would be an investigation, and I should stay out of it and in the end, if all was well, I could return to work. I was on paid administrative leave. Nothing turned up against me, and according to my attorney, I was cleared to return to work. Remember now, I was on leave and had not been fired. I called Atty. Appolonia and told him what I knew. He verified the information with Art Capaldi, the town solicitor. Felix also talked with Edouard Jacques, then town council president, who told him I was not to go back to my office.

Felix came back with, "Are you telling me the chief has to reapply for his job?"

"Yes, I guess so," was Jacques' reply.

I never received, nor did Felix, a formal directive stating I was not to return to work.

Felix called me and told me what happened and said, "To hell with them, the council and especially Jacques is wrong and they can't do that. Go back to work".

"Just like that," I asked?

"Just go."

"OK," I said and the following day I spent behind my old desk and it felt so good. I paid particular attention to the reaction of my Captain, Victor Pajak. I knew he was panting for my job that had been promised to him by Jacques, after he got rid of me. Pajak didn't say much that day. In fact, he spent very little time around the station.

* * *

Back to the Superior court trial, Judge Giannini was the uncle of Art Capaldi. Capaldi was also the legal advisor to the town council and had just been intimidated by the attorney general. As I understand it, Capaldi and members of the town council were told to cooperate with the attorney general's investigation or he would find a way to make their lives miserable. They caved. No one was going to stick up for me. They were all playing "cover your ass." Apparently, Judge Giannini got a touch intimidated also. More CYA. I can't really prove that but I do remember Dan Shea, the old court clerk, knowing about the phone call to the judge from the attorney general.

Only one witness was called by my lawyer during the appeal hearing on the charge of insubordination. Felix raked Ed Jacques, then new town council president, over the coals while on the witness stand. Jacques portrayal of dumb and dumber apparently didn't peak any interest from the judge. He was one slimy, spineless, backstabbing SOB and he was even given credit for doing it so well. No, I do not blame my entire demise on Jacques, even though he was one of the leaders in the movement to oust me.

Once the decision was rendered in Superior court, my lawyer was pretty down in the mouth and about ready to give up. I guess I couldn't blame him.

My indictment was made public and Felix told me I needed a good criminal defense lawyer, as this was way over his head. That's when John Tramonti entered the scene.

* * *

A businessman and good friend came to my aid and remained by my side throughout the ordeal. I had known Phil Casacalenda for many years. Phil owned and ran an auto body repair business and struggled to pay his own bills at the time. He was bringing up a young son, Phil, Jr., all alone. Phil, Jr., was brought up in the old Italian task master tradition. Phil did one hell of a job. Phil, Jr. is still in business with his father to this day, and is quite a gentleman.

Phil, Sr. went out and contacted business owners and made numerous telephone calls, begging money for my defense fund. His goal was to raise $1,500 to give to my civil attorney. People who had known me for years agreed they would help, then ran and hid. Out of the total committed, Phil was actually able to collect about $250. Atty. Appolonia went through the $250 in a flash just in witness fees. After a time, Phil even became discouraged and, although he never abandoned me, he kind of backed off. Who could blame him? I sure didn't.

My wife and I joined Phil and Phil, Jr. recently at a local country club for lunch. Phil was now negotiating to purchase that club. Not bad for a guy who didn't have much more than I did when all of this happened. To me, he was the same old Phil, one of the very few that never changed. Thanks, Phil.

I don't mean to give the impression that everyone turned their backs on me. Many did, but I still had some friends who were there for me as life support.

Bill Morin was one of those that stood beside me, kind of holding me up. Bill and I were on the state police together. We served at several state police barracks at the same time. He was about seven years senior to me and a man's man, or better said, a trooper's trooper. Bill was about five foot nine, with a chiseled face, well conditioned body, and was the epitome of a cop. I also worked for Sergeant Morin as my patrol commander. Bill had recently retired as a Lieutenant, when my troubles began. He got a job just to keep himself busy, and wound up framing houses with me. I learned a great deal from Bill about police work, and plenty about life. He was my mentor and hero, although I never told him that. I should have.

After the appeal hearing on the insubordination case, Attorney Appolonia dropped me off at my car and I drove home alone.

In my solitude, and despair, I contemplated how I had arrived in this nightmare.

CHAPTER 12

In June, 1969, newspapers, and many other forms of media, reported the discovery of a local West Warwick bartender, found lying on the back seat of his Cadillac convertible, with half of his head missing. The car was parked on a back road in Sterling, Connecticut. Sterling borders the western Coventry, Rhode Island/ eastern Connecticut state line. No one in Coventry saw any connection to our town, and thought it was nothing more than a gangland style murder. The Connecticut state police were working closely with our Rhode Island state police, but neither organization had any clues. Although, as mentioned, Sterling was right next to Coventry, no one bothered to keep the local police in the loop.

In July, one of my sergeants stopped in to my office at about 11:30 in the morning. My secretary rang me and told me Sgt. Valliere was there, and would like to see me. She asked if I could talk with him for a moment.

"Send him right in," I replied.

Sgt. Valliere appeared in my office doorway. I invited him in and motioned toward a chair. I had placed Valliere in charge of my bureau of criminal identifi- cation (BCI), responsible for processing breaking and entering scenes, taking photographs and obtaining other necessary data. He was doing a good job learning his new craft. Larry Valliere was a good looking man, about six feet tall, and in good shape. He had a pleasant personality, but was known as a practical joker.

"What can I do for you, Larry?"

"Chief," he began, "I have something to tell you but I don't want to talk to you here. Do you suppose we could go for a ride or something?"

"Sure," I replied.

I told him I had a luncheon speaking engagement at the Rotary Club but would be back within the hour. "Would that be OK?" I asked.

Larry said that was fine, and would see me around 12:30 PM. I would come back to the station to pick him up. Sgt. Valliere was not acting unusual, nervous or anything. I left for my luncheon.

The day was dismal and hot. It had been drizzling all morning.

Sgt. Valliere was waiting for me on the top step at the police station entrance when I returned. He got into my unmarked town police car, and we headed out toward the remote west end of town.

I gave Valliere a half sideway glance, and asked what was on his mind. What was so important?

Sgt. Valliere began, "You remember the Caprio murder? You know, the bartender that got killed a few weeks ago".

I said, "Yes, obviously, you mean James Caprio, the small time hood".

"Yah, that's the guy," responded Valliere.

In my mind, I figured Valliere had some information concerning the murder and wanted some advice on what direction to follow. I was half right.

After a short hesitation, he calmly said "We did him in".

My heart sank!

"What does that mean, Larry? Did you give him a beating or something?"

I knew one of my patrol cars stopped Caprio the night he was killed, but all they did was give him an equipment ticket for a burned out tail light and supposedly let him go. The patrol officers reported it to me, and were sent up to state police headquarters to give their account of the story to detectives. One of the state police detectives, Detective Correia, was one of my former partners. We graduated from the state police academy together.

I heard nothing more of the incident from the state police detectives or my officers.

Sgt. Valliere went on, "We didn't beat him up, we blew his head off".

"You what???" I exploded!

Once again Valliere calmly restated, "We blew his head off".

"Oh, cut the bullshit. Who's we?" I was trying to stay calm. My stomach was in knots and I thought I was going to throw up.

Valliere replied, "Me, Ron Parenteau, Larry LeClair and Roger Lemoi".

Lawrence (Larry) Valliere had been a member of the police department since 1964 and was promoted to sergeant in May of 1968. He was presently in charge of the night division. Roger Lemoi had been on the department about a year and a half. Officer Ronald Parenteau had been on the department since December, 1968 and Officers Lawrence LeClair and Dennis Perry were still probationary patrol officers, which meant they had not completed six months, at the time.

Taking some deep breaths, trying to calm myself a bit, I said, "OK, start from the beginning". I was so full of disbelief, I could not possibly digest what he had just told me.

Larry Valliere began his story without a tinge of nervousness in his voice.

Ronnie Parenteau and Larry LeClair were in Joe's Diner, a popular Coventry diner. It was the place to be after a night out in the taverns. It seems Caprio, a bartender, came walking in with another male. Caprio walked past Officer Parenteau and made a smart remark. Parenteau ignored him. Ron Parenteau got up and walked over to the telephone to call his girlfriend. His girlfriend worked at the Doll House lounge where Caprio tended bar. Caprio knew Officer Parenteau was dating the waitress and didn't like that he was interested in her, too.

"Go on," I said to Sgt. Valliere.

"Well, Ron said something to his girl about Caprio getting it that night and there was going to be trouble. Then Parenteau and LeClair left the diner. As they were leaving, they saw Roger Lemoi and Dennis Perry, in another police cruiser, as they pulled into the diner parking lot".

"Was Perry involved in this, too?" I asked.

"No," Valliere said, "We told him to screw. He went back on patrol."

Valliere went on, "I pulled up in a plain plate cruiser, and Parenteau told me what was going on".

"What was going on?" I wanted to know!

"You'll see," said Valliere.

Valliere continued, "Caprio left the diner and was followed by Lemoi and LeClair. Parenteau left alone in another cruiser".

"Then what"?

"Well, Roger Lemoi stopped Caprio and put him in the rear seat of his cruiser and drove him to Cardi's sand bank off Arnold Road in eastern Coventry". (Pretty remote in those days.)

"There was me," Valliere said, "LeClair, Parenteau and Lemoi in the sand bank. We were just going to give him a good beating for fooling around with Ronnie's broad, but Caprio told us that we could do whatever we wanted, but when he got out of the hospital he would get each and every one of us. After hearing that, LeClair pulled out his service revolver and was going to shoot him right then and there. I told him not to because they would trace the bullet to a thirty eight, and all cops carried thirty eight revolvers. So, Valliere went on, 'I told them to keep him there and I would be right back'."

Larry Valliere said he drove back to the station and got one of the sawed off shot guns, and brought it back to the sand bank.

"We decided we didn't want to shoot him in Coventry, so we moved to Gillespie's sand bank just over the line in West Greenwich," Valliere continued.

"Who saw you take the shot gun out of the station?" I asked.

Valliere replied that Al Lameroux, the night desk man, saw him walk out with the gun but didn't pay much attention to him. "We were always fooling around with the guns and taking them out at night," Valliere added. "I also took some shot gun shells. I handed the shot gun to LeClair and Lemoi gave him a couple of shells".

"And then," I prodded?

"Well, Caprio said he wanted to take a leak and we told him to go ahead. He walked a little ways away and stopped. I never saw anyone piss that long in my life. Then I told him to kneel down. I just looked at LeClair and he walked over and put the gun to the back of Caprio's head. I told him to hold it. Christ, at that range he would have blown him all over the place. Back up. LeClair backed up about four feet and raised the gun. Then he mumbled something and pulled the trigger. Caprio fell over dead".

I was beyond being stunned!

I looked directly at Sgt. Valliere and, although I was driving, I wanted to arrest him right then and there. But instead, I said again, "Larry, cut the shit, now where did you ever come up with a story like that?" I was praying it wasn't true. I didn't want to let myself believe they had done this.

"No shit, Chief, I mean it. Me and Lemoi stuffed him in the back of his car, and Lemoi drove the car to Connecticut to dump it and the body. I took off and went back to the station. Parenteau and LeClair followed Lemoi in their police cruiser to bring Lemoi back".

Valliere went on, "We planned to leave the car in a picnic area just over the line, but when they got there someone was parking, and the guys panicked, and dumped the car in the first driveway they saw. Then the guys came back to Coventry and Lemoi went back on patrol".

"Why are you telling me all of this now," I asked Valliere?

"Because you keep telling us you will support us and we knew you would back us up," Valliere answered.

"How in the hell do you conceal a murder," I asked?

He laughed, "I knew you would say something like that. Oh well, you can believe it or not."

Valliere made it quite clear that I had nothing more than this conversation with him. No proof or evidence and certainly, no confession. He stated they had all sworn a blood oath that none of them would confess to anything, and they had a great deal of faith, believing I would not turn on them.

He was right, of course. It frustrated the hell out of me. The entire episode changed my life in a heartbeat.

I could not dismiss Valliere's story. I thought of driving to state police headquarters and talking with my old detective commander James (Moon) Mullen. I knew exactly what the detectives would do, and immediately, proof or no proof. The state police kind of looked down on local police and considered themselves superior. I don't know, maybe they were. Obviously, that is why I wanted to be a state trooper and not a local cop. Kind of like the CIA not liking the FBI and vice-versa. Actually we thought local cops were just plain dumb, in many cases, and couldn't find their asses with either hand. Well, now I was one of the locals and I was determined

I was not going to tip my hand and blow this investigation, at least not yet.

I dropped sergeant Valliere at his car and went back to my office.

To insure the information Valliere had just given me, I typed a short story of what had transpired between Sgt. Valliere and me. I mentioned all of the names in this communication. I put the story in a plain white envelope and placed it in my desk, pretty well hidden and locked the drawer. I called Lieutenant Andy Wallace into my office and explained to him that there was "something" in an envelope in my drawer, and should anything happen to me, he was to go to my desk, break the lock if necessary, and find the envelope. The contents of the envelope would tell him what he needed to know. He didn't question me. Lieutenant Wallace was an army reserve major, with a balding head. He was about six feet tall, in really good shape and squared away, at all times. He had a small mustache that actually looked like it belonged on him, even though I didn't approve of extra facial hair. I never bothered him or asked him to shave. I had absolute faith in his not sharing our conversation with anyone. He didn't. I waited a couple of weeks and nothing out of the ordinary happened. There were no breaks and no hard evidence from any source.

The evening of Valliere's admission, I waited for Stan Jendzejec to arrive in my office, as was his routine.

In addition to Wallace knowing about the envelope in my desk, when Stan arrived, I also told him.

I related the entire story to Stan and told him I didn't think it was wise for him, or any of the council members, to become involved. After some consideration, I made a decision not to tell Capaldi as I knew he would have been duty bound to reveal the information.

I can't be specific enough about having no proof, and nothing concrete to go on. Valliere's oratory was not a confession, so what exactly did I have? The answer, nothing!

In mid July the town council decided to throw a party for town employees. Several police officers, allegedly involved in the murder, attended with their wives. I was there, and watched the officers closely. Roger Lemoi, in particular, got drunk and passed out. This was unusual because I knew he didn't drink. That was my first indication that something was seriously wrong. Of course, I suspected I knew what.

About the same time I sent another of the officers, allegedly involved, to breathalyzer school at the University of Rhode Island. Officer Dennis Perry was on patrol the night of the murder, but supposedly knew nothing about it. Dennis was simply told to stand guard at the entrance of the sand bank, but allegedly, did not know what was going on. Officer Perry was told if anyone came he was just to shoo them away. He did as he was ordered, and took up a blocking post at the entrance to the sand bank.

After the murder while Perry was in the breathalyzer training class, something occurred that gave me pause. The students have to drink a certain amount of alcohol, to learn how the breathalyzer would work on them. Perry got drunk to such a degree that it took oxygen to revive him! I was becoming more and more convinced the bubble was about to burst.

I felt it was time to convey my thoughts to another member of my police department and that was detective Carl Brown.

I shared with Carl what information I had and told him to snoop around but to be very, very discreet.

In the meantime I was working late one evening. I was down in my office and Tom Jones asked to come in and speak with me. I said sure, and invited him in. I motioned him toward a chair, but Tom remained standing rocking nervously from one foot to another.

"Chief," he began, "You remember the Caprio murder?"

Christ, I thought, he can't be involved too.

"Yes," I answered, "What's up?" I was trying to be as casual as I could.

"Well, I think some of our guys had something to do with it".

"What makes you say that, Tom"?

"I have been riding around with Parenteau and, on several occasions, I would begin talking about the murder, and Ronnie gets all upset".

Tom went on, "The other night I was with him until about three in the morning, and he kept pumping me as to what I knew. I told him not much, but I do know Caprio was playing around with the same girl you're seeing. Anyway, Parenteau told me to keep my nose clean or I might get seriously hurt".

If these men were all involved in a murder what would one more mean, even if it is a fellow police officer?

That did it, I realized. I couldn't wait any longer.

"Thanks Tom," I said and Jones left.

CHAPTER 13

I had this sinking feeling that there had to be some basis for Valliere's bizarre story, or confession if you will. It was time to move, before someone else got hurt. I heard Officer LeClair got himself mixed up with a local waitress and his wife, or girlfriend, whoever she was, found out and got all over him. Complaints about LeClair's behavior were coming to me. I directed my two lieutenants to investigate. They concluded LeClair had broken all kinds of departmental rules and regulations. I called officer LeClair into my officer. Both lieutenants were there with me. We apprised him of the charges that would likely be brought against him. I learned just about everyone on the department had known of LeClair's antics and transgressions. I had to maintain discipline over all of the men, and I couldn't let him get away with this. He reluctantly offered to resign, if I wouldn't push the matter. I was still not certain of his role in the murder and wanted to be sure he would be around when we needed him. He submitted his resignation, and we were able to get him another position locally.

My conversation with Tom Jones kept ringing in my head. I knew I had to do something about it. There was no concrete proof, but I had to play a hunch, a feeling down deep in my gut, told me someone was ready to crack.

I got home at about three in the morning and called my former state police detective commander, Captain Jimmy Mullen. Captain Mullen was a straight laced, bright and, very professional, detective commander. I liked him. I told him what I had learned and that there was a strong possibility some of my men were responsible for the murder. The captain asked if I could be at headquarters the first thing in the morning to meet with him and the Colonel. I was there at seven fifteen AM.

Captain Mullin, Colonel Stone and I met in the superintendants office. I explained what I knew and what Valliere had told me. I also explained I had a couple of my people snooping around and staying close to the suspected police officers. I gave a typewritten statement to an old academy classmate, Eddie Corrier, and signed the statement. That was usual policy, for as long as I can remember.

As expected, a few hours later, state police detectives swooped down on my police officers and apprehended all of them, with the exception of Lawrence LeClair, who was vacationing with his family in Ohio. After a few days, he received word, and agreed to turn himself in.

All of the officers were arrested, taken to state police headquarters and questioned by detectives. Obviously, I kept members of my department out of the investigation. I worried one misstep by the Coventry police department could cause questions of one kind or another. Just what that might have been, I had no idea, but I wasn't taking any chances. I did not want to give the impression that my involvement would taint the investigation in any manner.

Remember now, it was rumored that I was trying to cover this crime up. It should also be remembered, that no one would have known anything unless I told them.

As I was to learn, one of the officers broke down, and admitted what had happened that night when James Caprio was stopped and eventually murdered. That was enough for the state police to substantiate the charges of murder and accessory to murder. Numerous other lesser charges were added. Standard procedure.

Four suspended officers pled guilty to second degree murder, and were given twenty five year sentences. I compliment my former state police associates for conducting a thorough investigation that left no stone unturned, while building the case and follow-up prosecution. All things considered, these men would probably serve one third of their sentences and begin a new life. James Caprio had no chance at a new life.

There was a defense attorney named Daniels that made a statement that he could not wait to get me on the stand during the trial. He told me that personally. I told him to do his best. The day came in superior court when it was my time on the witness stand and I was to be questioned. Attorney Daniels had his crack at me. He tried his best to make me look like a fool, but the judge shut him down early, and often, until, frustrated, he shut his mouth and sat down. The judge's name was Christopher Del Sesto, former governor of the state of Rhode Island. He was a good governor, and a good superior court judge, in a state known for its heavy criminal mafia ties. At one point, I obviously did not answer a question the way he thought I should or hesitated and didn't respond quickly enough, and the judge reacted with, "I think the chief is lying." I was a little distraught at that response but I kept my cool. This was one battle I couldn't win under the conditions. I didn't need a contempt citation thrown at me. I stared back at the judge. Glared, is probably more like it. I was told I could step down.

Unquestionably, the judge felt I was trying the shield my former police officers and perhaps even conceal some facts. He was right about half his feelings. I would have protected them with all I had, but I would not have lied to cover up for them. My former cops knew that.

Finally, all four pleaded guilty and the proceedings were over. It was not over for me, however.

CHAPTER 14

Since the four officers were charged, morale was at an all time low. Needless to say, members of the department were pretty distraught with all that happened and just about no one was on top of their game.

Each year, the police department was one of the marching units in the annual Old Home Days festival, usually, leading the parade off. This was a voluntary function. If the men do march they don't get paid for overtime work. Word reached me that no one was going to march this year. I needed to do something to bring these guys back.

I typed a memo:

To all members of the Coventry Police Department:

As has been the tradition of the police department for many years, we are once again invited to participate in the annual Old Home Days parade. Obviously, recent events have dulled some member's enthusiasm.

I understand.

I will hold no ill feelings if you do not show up at the starting position, but I have enough pride in this department and respect for you, that I will be at the starting position, at the appointed time, and will carry our departmental flag in one hand and our nations flag in the other, if I have to. If any of you would care to accompany me, it would be greatly appreciated.

On the morning of the parade, I drove into Parente's gas station, the starting point for the parade. Huddled in a group in the lot was every member of the police department. My eyes welled up with tears and my heart pounded. My God, I thought, they're all here. Truth is I had a very strong gut feeling they would be. I personally went around and shook their hands and thanked them. A couple of them said "No chief, thank you". Wow!

The parade started and we stepped off. I was up front and to the right. As we passed a large stone wall on the right hand side of the street, I noticed some young teenage boys sitting atop the wall.

Suddenly, this cat call rang out from one of the buys, "Hey Chief, where are your machine guns?" Praise the Lord for professional policemen. My men just looked straight ahead and followed me without a glance at the punk. He got enough boo's from the crowd. In the old days, he would have been dragged off the wall and slapped around by the cops.

This was not the old days.

Our parade route was about three miles long and I was in disbelief with every step.

When I was in the Marine Corps, I participated in a parade down Biscayne Boulevard in Miami Beach, Florida. As the marines passed the viewing stand the band struck up the Marine Corps hymn. The crowd rose and started applauding and yelling encouragement to the marines. I had chills and I am sure I wasn't the only marine that did. That parade day in Coventry, Rhode Island in 1969 easily rivaled that day in Miami Beach. Spectators lined the main drag of Washington

St. every step of the way, for more than three miles. As the police department came into view, the residents and viewers got up on their feet, yelled and shouted encouragement; things like "God Bless you," "We're with you," and "Chief you're doing a great job". It was amazing to say the least. One of my best childhood friends, Carl Fusaro, came off the sidewalk and gave me a big hug as the parade was passing by. Hadn't seen him in years. What a great guy, with so many feelings and emotions. Italians can be like that. We are still friends. He is a professor of music in Kansas City.

Amid all the tragedy, what a glorious day. Folks can say what they want but when real adversity hits you hard, the honest, hardworking people will be there to prop you up.

During the months to come, I did some things I wished I hadn't. For example, some large super markets lobbied state legislators to introduce a bill that would stop little mom and pop grocery stores from selling meat on Sunday's. In other words the "big guys" could sell anything they wanted, but the little owner had better not or they could be arrested and fined. I was interviewed by a local reporter and asked what my feelings were about the Sunday Meat Sales Law. I candidly said I didn't think the law was fair, and I was not going to order my cops to patrol the small variety stores and arrest people for selling a pound of hamburger or even a steak on Sunday.

Big mistake! The attorney general of the state did not like that at all. I guess he felt that some little local yokel police chief was not going to defy the state law.

That was not at all my intention, but I had no defense, and I was going to pay for that later. This episode kind of started the laundry list of things that would mount against me, until they found something substantial, whether I made a mistake or not. I had no idea at the time what these gutter sniping, back stabbing, self serving public officials could do. They have resources, secret procedures and investigators John Q. Public does not have. Many times, they tried a number of these techniques on me. One honest judge put a clamp on them. Remember Judge Giannini?

CHAPTER 15

I knew, or at least I should have known, there would be suspicion as to whether or not I was trying to cover up the murder. Truth is, the thought never crossed my mind. To be asked, even many years later does not cause me to falter or wonder. As a matter of fact, no one has ever really come right out and asked me, "Would you have covered up this murder if you could have?" Rumor and innuendo are a terrible thing. My answer would have been, and is, No, I would not!

Speaking of rumor, one evening I was guest speaker for the local Lions Club. I finished my talk and stopped at the bar to say hello to the bartender and golfing friend. He gave me a glass of tonic water. No booze. We talked for a few minutes, and I then sat at a lounge table with a couple of councilmen. About fifteen minutes later, excused myself and went directly home.

The following morning, a gentleman I had never met asked to speak with me and I told my desk man to send him down to my office. I would later come to learn, he was characterized as the town drunk. This particular morning, however, he was as sober as a judge. I got up from my desk, walked over to him and shook his hand. I asked what I could do for him. He said he was there to apologize. A little surprised, I asked,

"Apologize for what?"

"Well," he began, "Last night I was at Joe's Diner when you were speaking to the Lions Club".

"Go on," I said.

He continued, "I saw you go into the lounge, talk with the bartender and I heard you order a plain tonic water."

"So?" I responded.

The man continued, "I saw you sit with the council men and then leave. I got into my car and followed you home. You put your car in that tiny garage and then I saw you go into the house. I waited for a short time to see if you would come out again, or anyone would come to see you. Nothing happened and I drove off.

"So what's the apology?" I asked.

The alleged town drunk went on to say, "I have been accused of a lot of things, and so have you, but last night I watched you for the greater part of the evening and you never did anything wrong. I heard you were driving like a crazy drunk, and was all over the road. You got stopped in Westerly up at the Connecticut line and were taken to the Westerly police station and locked in a padded cell until you sobered up. That wasn't possible considering I had my eye on you for most of the evening. I'm here to apologize because if I had not seen you, I would have probably believed the "RUMOR". With that, he got up, excused himself, and walked out of my office. I never had occasion to see or run into him again.

CHAPTER 16

I should explain at this point, when all of this started, Richard Isreal was not the Attorney General of the state of Rhode Island. He was a lawyer by the name of Herbert F. De Simone. It was through his office that the investigation of the Coventry police department had begun. He had a job to do and if there was something going on in law enforcement, he, being the chief law enforcement officer in the state, should conduct an investigation. I knew that, and publicly welcomed it. Certainly, we had nothing to hide. Mr. DeSimone had a chief investigator by the name of Cappamachio who was a former FBI agent and an attorney.

I was never interviewed by Mr. Cappamaccio but he did talk to members of my police department. The next thing I knew he called a grand jury together and called in members of the police department to testify.

He did not call me.

I was to learn from some of the police officers that had testified before the grand jury that they were being eaten alive in that grand jury room. They were being insulted, threatened and intimidated. I couldn't just blow that off. I called the attorney general's office in Providence and learned the attorney general was at his summer residence in the posh resort area of Narragansett, Rhode Island. I was told he was too busy, and didn't have time for me. I made it clear that he either talk to me, or read my remarks of his tactics in the news media. I had a television broadcaster friend who wanted to put me on the air. Once Mr. DeSimone grasped what I was saying, he invited me to his summer home.

I asked Sergeant Tom Holt, my mid-evening desk commander, to come with me to DeSimone's cottage. Upon entering the kitchen area, I was greeted by Attorney General DeSimone, Mr. Cappamaccio and several other suited gentlemen all looking professional grade. I got immediately to the point and told him I did not think it was fair to tear up my entire police department over a crime they had no involvement in, and did not know anything about. I reminded him that at the time of the arrests, I was the one who told my former state police detective colleagues. Members of my department knew nothing about the crime, although a couple of them had some inkling. I certainly did not want to interfere with the attorney general's investigation, but I also did not want my police officers torn to shreds either.

Mr. DeSimone thanked me for coming, and said he would talk with Mr. Cappamaccio, who was standing right there the whole time. I allowed myself to think I had done the right thing. Probably the wrong thing was to threaten to go to the media, but I said it anyway. I should have known I wasn't going to get away with that. After all, I was only a thirty four year old brash "hick" police chief. Would I do it all over again? YES!

As soon as the grand jury was reconvened, the tenor of the proceedings changed dramatically.

Mr. Cappamaccio reportedly treated the members of the police department much differently. The grand jury ended abruptly and findings of that grand jury were that no one other than the arrested police officers were involved in anything abnormal or unprofessional. They concluded that I had done nothing wrong and there was no malfeasance of my office.

Shortly after the investigation was over, things were getting back to normal. Attorney General DeSimone was named the next secretary of the United States Department of Transportation. I was happy for him. It appeared he put a damper on the mean spirited Cappamaccio.

Around the same time, I got a very interesting telephone call from a well known local lady, someone I had known since I was a teenager. She was very pretty, and a very classy person, coming from a fairly prominent background. I don't know how she knew what was going on in the grand jury with my police officers, and their degradation and intimidation, but she did. She also knew I went to Narragansett to defend my men. She never told me how she knew all of this, but she was right on the nose. Her statement stills rings in my ears.

"If you ever have a problem with Herb DeSimone, you call me right away." On more than one occasion we spent a little snuggle time together. He probably wouldn't want that to get around."

Could that have been the reason for the attitude change in the grand jury? Did someone on the grand jury know her and call her? The possibilities were limitless. I was just happy she was there when I needed a friend. Best I can say to her is thanks for whatever you did.

Now comes the giant slayer Richard Isreal. He is the worm that took over from Mr. DeSimone and he had ambitions to become governor of the state of Rhode Island.

CHAPTER 17

Finally, in August, 1969. my probationary period was over. All of the councilmen agreed to swear me in as permanent police chief. There was, however, one councilman who made known that he was not in favor of my appointment but would vote for my confirmation. That man was Edouard Jacques.

"Gentlemen, what is your pleasure?" Stanley Jendzejec asked.

Al Frechette, our town solicitor wasn't going to let this circus pass by without him offering his two cents worth.

Frechette wheezed out, "I have checked the law and I find in my legal interpretation that we must either appoint this man permanent or fire him. The provision under the police act requires this."

Baloney, I thought. I read the act and there was no such thing in it. There wasn't even a provision for a six month probationary period. This was merely at the whim of the town council. I figured Frechette had the people pretty well snowed and the opposition had no legal mind with them at the meeting so they had to accept what Frechette said. No one argued.

Councilman Reggie Mailloux (May-you) said, "Mr. President, I make a motion that we appoint Harvey C. Simmons as our permanent police chief."

Councilman Harvey Forrest seconded the motion.

Stanley intoned, "All those in favor signify by saying aye."

All of the councilmen echoed "aye" in unison.

The auditorium went wild.

Everyone came to their feet whistling, yelling, clapping, and slapping each other on the back.

I got up out of my seat in the center of the auditorium and headed for the stage taking the aisle to the right. I was shaking hands and being slapped on the back, kissed and hugged. My mother was in the audience, just to the right front of me on the other side of the aisle in an end seat. Mom had a big, broad smile on her face and as I saw her I stopped and lifted her out of her seat and gave her a big hug and a kiss, and told her I loved her. I wanted her to be proud of her youngest son. She had tears in her twinkling Irish blue eyes, and said "I've always been proud of you." At that moment my heart was so full. Could all of this be happening to me, I wondered? Mom kissed my cheek and gave me a little shove and whispered, "Go now, go be our chief of police."

I stepped up onto the stage. The applause still hadn't subsided. People were on their feet all over the auditorium. Even some of the opposition submitted and I saw a few of them clapping. What a thrill! One I had never known before . . . . one I would probably never know again.

I took the oath of office and thunderous applause greeted me again. I had what I came for, the support of the people. All in all, it was one hell of a glorious evening. Thinking back now, the question arises, where did all of the happiness, dedication and support go? How quickly, a few moments of glory can dwindle. How quickly, all of this can be destroyed; a career, a life. I knew what it was like from both sides. I came in like the mighty proud lion but was beaten up and thrown out by many of the same people. I learned what it was like to be in the center of the arena awaiting the attacks of hungry mad dogs. You've heard of the birth and will follow along toward the demise of a police chief.

CHAPTER 18

Months passed like weeks. It was the fall of 1969. The work was long and hard, much harder than I thought it would be. I learned a great deal. I had to reason with disgruntled officers. I had to get to know these men. I had to just about live with them, get to know their families, laugh with them, to share their problems both personal and professional. I sent flowers to sick wives. I visited disabled officers in their homes and in the hospital if that was necessary. I sent small presents when babies were born. I went to wakes when a relative died. I spoke at testimonials and other festive occasions. I sat on police hearing boards when police members violated a rule or regulation. My fingers were in everything. I wanted to know what was going on now, not a day later. I got out of bed some nights and went to private homes when a department member had a problem. Many times, I might not have been able to help, but I was there just in case I could assist. I promised the officers that whatever happened, their plight would remain between me and them. I would tell no one I was there.

I was called to the scene of fatal accidents. I talked with my officers on patrol on long lonely nights. I brought them coffee. I gave them a little extra time at Thanksgiving and Christmas to enjoy a meal with their families. I allowed the desk sergeant to go home while I handled the desk. Hell, most of the time I didn't have a family anyway. I didn't ask any thanks, nor did I expect any. The guys responded by giving the residents of the town of Coventry one of the finest police departments in New England and it seemed like everyone else knew that too. The day of the "Keystone Kops" was gone.

A brief side story about the "good old days" is one when a friend was locked up one night

Joey Muschiano, Jr. is a story in and of itself. Joey was a barber by trade. His father, Joe, Sr., was a nice man who taught his son the profession. Joey learned well and eventually took over the business when his father moved to Arizona. Joey did me some favors when I needed help, and a place to live back when I was on the state police. I stayed at Joey's house and we had our share of fun.

I do believe Joey fashioned himself a small time gangster. He liked hanging where the hoods hung and he liked acting like a little tough guy. To picture Joey Muschiano, visualize Sammy Davis, Jr., only a shade lighter, and you have a carbon copy of Joseph P. Muschiano, Jr.

On this particular night, I returned to the station, and headed down to my office. I had to walk by the entrance to the cell block and glanced in. Lo and behold, there's Joey sitting on a jail cell cot.

I walked into the cell block and Joey greeted me at the bars.

I asked, "Joey, what the hell are you doing here?"

"Just a little scuffle," Joey replied. Then he said, "Just let me the hell out of here."

I told him I just couldn't do that without finding out what happened, and the officer's side of the story. I turned and started to walk out to go back upstairs and learn what had happened. As I turned, Joey called me back,

"Hey," he said, "you want to take this with you?"

Joey was dangling a small handgun in the bars, holding it out for me to take. It was loaded.

I grabbed the weapon out of his hand, and snarled, "I'll be right back."

I bounded up the stairs and back into the patrol office. I was seething.

"Who brought Muschiano in?"

The desk sergeant just looked at me and said he would call the patrol officer in.

I told the desk sergeant to get the keys to the cell and politely go down and unlock Joey and release him.

"Bring him up here," I ordered.

When the arresting officer gets here, you have him give Mr. Muschiano a ride home and apologize for any inconvenience you might have caused him.

The sergeant just looked at me wanting to ask why? Before he could ask the question I slammed the revolver down on the sergeant's desk and said,

"Unload this and give it back to him, and you better pray to God he doesn't go around blabbing about what goddamned fools he just made out of you guys." Do you have any idea what this could have resulted in? No one even searched him?" I was so mad I was shaking.

Fortunately, nothing more was said and the incident ended quietly. Could be Joey was still my friend and wouldn't sink the department with a story like this.

Keystone Kops, huh?

* * *

Residents appeared to be satisfied by overwhelmingly supporting a policeman's ball. The event had not been held for years because no one ever went to it. I thought it would be a good idea to re-establish a committee, and see if we could hold a ball. In the three policeman's balls I attended, we raised between six and seven thousand dollars for the police officers' fund. The events were packed. I didn't spend much time at the affairs, because I didn't think it was right for me to be seen hovering over bottles of beer and mixed drinks. Besides, this was a party for the guys and not for me.

We had to hold the event in the neighboring town since there was nothing large enough in our town. Ticket sales told us that.

Finally, the men had enough money to rent the upper level of an old automobile dealership in the east end of town. The guys called their club "The Pig Pen." Clever! I had nothing to do with that.

The monthly rent was really a gift from the owner of the building. It was very inexpensive. The guys got together and remodeled the upper level into a very nice meeting hall. I didn't spend much time there, because this was their club and it would not have been right for me in my position. One thing I did right. Had I hung out there, I would be able to hear the rumors ringing to this day; hey the chief's getting plastered nights with his guys. Hell, they had me involved in the murder, didn't they?

I decided that a special award should be made each year to an outstanding police officer. To my dismay, the town council president learned about it from "The Mouth," Lieutenant Victor Pajak.

As long as we could establish an award at this level, it really didn't matter to me who sponsored it. A plaque was awarded at a regular town council meeting and the police officer's family was in attendance, along with a smattering of press and, of course, comrades. I did get to name the man; Pajak couldn't take that away. Stanley Jendzejec made some minor political statements, but the award served the purpose and helped to encourage the officers.

The men were molded into, not a good police department, but a great one, and I was their leader. I had a feeling they knew how I felt about them, and in return I believed they had a genuine good feeling about me. Leadership has to be earned, not demanded, or commanded. If you can't walk the walk or talk the talk, you aren't going to be effective.

CHAPTER 19

On more than one occasion, I would return to the office during the evening to mediate quarrels between neighbors who just couldn't get along with one another. Getting into one of these confrontations can become real dicey, usually because one or the other party wants you on their side, and you have to remain as neutral as possible. Good luck with that. In the end, they wind up ganging up on the mediator. No matter if they go home satisfied and can get along.

Much of the western side of Coventry is very rural and remote. There are some smaller beautiful lakes and, of course, with the water comes small homes and cabins. Like most areas throughout the country, there is a fairly good sized increase in summer population. Some of the residents have winterized their dwellings and made them year-round homes. No one in law enforcement had ever paid much attention to the full time homes or the vacant summer cabins. This created a real haven for burglars. We would have a fair number of break-ins and criminal damage.

In an attempt to reduce the potential threat of breaking and entering, I decided to assign regular patrols to these areas. Police presence, seen even once in awhile, was better than none at all. I decided to hold several meetings with the citizens to consider the possibility of raising funds to purchase some type of vehicle that could adequately access and patrol these remote recreational areas.

The first such meeting was held at a YMCA camp out in the woods. An area beautifully kept with beaches, baseball fields, sleeping accommodations and other related services. We met in a room adjacent to the dining hall. It didn't take long getting to the crux of the matter and of course, that was money. I told the group the police department did not have cruisers built strong enough to patrol the dirt roads strewn with rocks and boulders. Keep in mind, there were no civilian four-wheel drive vehicles back then. Someone asked what we would need. I replied that a military style, four-wheel drive vehicle would do nicely. Something that could get stranded homeowners out in really foul weather, snow, ice and assist in getting folks their groceries, medicines and other important necessities.

The idea caught on and the group agreed we needed something. That evening small donations of five, ten and twenty dollars were made and we collected nearly one hundred dollars. The following day I opened a bank account. The only people that could make withdrawals would be me, my executive officer and then there had to be three signatures. We got a female member of the group to agree to be a signer.

Does all of this sound like it's going too well? Hang on!

It was later I decided to hold a dance to raise more funds. A local civic club in western Coventry offered its facility for the affair. The club would hold two hundred and fifty people. A group of nice ladies formed a committee and decorated the hall. I had the tickets printed through our town sergeant, Frank Iuliano, at his cost. Some posters were made at the local high school in the art class. The kids did a great job for us. Tickets were distributed to all of the police officers and the auxiliary (volunteer) police officers to sell.

There was a minor struggle going on between me, as the chief, and the auxiliary police leader, Joseph Wilkicki. Wilkicki thought he could run his own little private police department and didn't have to work within the framework of the actual police department.

This part of the story kind of breaks into the fund raising effort but it is important enough to enter here.

* * *

Back in the fall of '69, the auxiliary were an untrained group of volunteers who would travel with our regular police officers, especially during the evenings. Not unusual in small rural towns throughout the country. These men, or most of them, were appointed before I was the chief. Townspeople knew many of them as constables. There had been no firearm training or safety courses, no knowledge of criminal or motor vehicle law and really no knowledge of law enforcement whatsoever. I was opposed to this group and they did little to enhance the image of our department. Here's one glowing example of a host of situations that existed.

An older town resident was out on the road one afternoon and noticed what he thought was a motor vehicle violation and being a constable or auxiliary, he decided to do something about it. This seventy plus year old gentleman was successful in getting the motorist stopped by flashing his badge and gun at the driver. Apparently, he gave this "young fella" a good ass-chewing and sent him on his way with the classic statement, "Don't let me catch you doing this around here anymore." I knew his heart was in the right place but I had to put a stop to this.

Word came back to me instantly, Oh, my God, I thought. Someone could get killed here. I ordered my lieutenant to get this man's constable badge and gun, and return them to me immediately, and advise this gentleman his services would no longer be required by our police department. The lieutenant told him and the old fellow responded with,

"You tell that whipper snapper police chief to take this badge and pin it to his ass, I wouldn't work for him anyhow."

That little incident got back to the auxiliary leader and he demanded a confrontation with me. It amounted to him telling me that he would handle any complaints about "his men," and I should just keep my nose out of his department.

"Your what?" I demanded.

"You heard me" Wilkicki answered and walked out the door.

I explained the situation to the councilmen and the police committee, and immediately got them behind me for the sake of safety, the operation and good order of the police department. They agreed except there was one naysayer; yes, you guessed it Edouard Jacques.

An official department order was issued and posted the following morning. The auxiliary police department was to be disbanded and none would be allowed to ride in the police cruisers or participate in any kind of police activity until further notice.

Some time later, I did install another police auxiliary. They did receive training, and they had to qualify with their weapons according to state law and standards. We actually did make them a useful part of the police department, but it took awhile. I never did win Wilkicki over, but he cooperated and we got along.

Back to the dance.

Tickets were distributed, but I learned the auxiliary police officers held a meeting and decided they would not sell any tickets, and tried to "sandbag" our success in raising funds. They asked everyone they could, not to participate in ticket sales tickets so the police chief would fall flat on his ass. I learned of this the morning of the dance. Hardly any tickets had been sold. I called several of my police officers and had them come to my home. I established teams and assigned them certain areas to cover, and sent them out to local businesses and to others. All in all, we sold over two hundred tickets over the telephone that day. To say the least, the dance was a total success. We raised more than seven hundred dollars after expenses. This money was placed in the account and a balance of more than eleven hundred dollars was established. We were, however, still a distance away from purchasing an adequate vehicle.

I had an idea and wrote a letter to the Secretary of the Navy, the Honorable John H.Chaffee, also the former governor of the state of Rhode Island. He was a Korean war veteran and a Marine Corps captain. So was I.

When I was a state trooper, I had the tragic honor of being an honor guard at his teenage daughter's funeral. She was thrown from a horse and then stomped to death.

Prior to my contact with Secretary Chaffee, I called Quonset Point Naval Air station supply depot and asked if they might have a retired Jeep the town might obtain. They had hundreds of old military vehicles in surplus just rotting away out in a field. I saw them. I was told, in no uncertain terms, they couldn't help me and just blew me off. My phone call was abruptly terminated.

Several days after the letter was sent, I received a telephone call from Secretary Chaffee himself. Mr. Secretary told me to go to the naval air station. I would be met at the gate and allowed to choose whichever surplus vehicle I wanted.

A day after the call from the naval secretary I took my executive officer and went to Quonset Point. You would not have believed the reception we got at the main gate. One might have thought the president was coming. A marine detachment was there as an escort, as was the procurement officer for the surplus inventory; same guy that hung up on me a few days prior. He was all full of smiles and manners this day. To top it all off, the base commander introduced himself and offered to guide us through the process. I told him we really appreciated that, but we would be fine. He saluted and backed away with a big smile on his face.

We picked out a Jeep that looked kind of rough but ran very well and reportedly did not need a lot of work. We came away with a functioning Jeep. Funny what one letter can do. They even threw in an extra motor for spare parts.

The Jeep was assigned to its designated area in the western portion of the town and concentrated mainly on back roads and remote areas. I didn't have any problem assigning men to drive the Jeep, at least for a time; a very short time. It was a new toy and the men tired of it quickly. In the end, we assigned the vehicle to the auxiliary police, who by now, learned and accepted the fact they had one police chief, me. The poor Jeep wouldn't run two nights in a row. They would do things like blow the clutch because they wanted to drive like John Wayne in Sands of Iwo Jima. The windshield was broken and the seats ripped. Finally, I asked my friend Tom Kenahan, the highway superintendant, if he wanted it. He threw a small plow on it and the Jeep ran for years, and was still going when I left the department.

Here it comes now . . . . wait for it!

One afternoon three gracious ladies and two gentlemen came to my office and demanded to know what happened to the Jeep, or at least what happened to all of the money they raised? "They raised?" I thought. I did not choose to confront them so I showed them all of our records of all the repair receipts covering every bill we ever had. The group was shown the remaining bank balance. I was satisfied the entire process was as legitimate as it could get. I did not get closely involved in the financial transactions and never did make a withdrawal. My

executive office, Paul Green, handled all of the department's financial matters from budgets to dispersing any
type of funds. Paul was a fine gentleman and I trusted
him completely.

I thought our little group of concerned citizens and
muck-rakers were satisfied. How many times can I be
wrong?

With the Jeep gone and no money in the regular
police budget to obtain anything better, I learned there
was some equipment that had been purchased for the
department but not completely paid for. The items
included a 3M copy machine, a duplicating machine and
an electric typewriter. I talked this over with our financial expert and advisor and he decided to borrow the
money from the Jeep account and pay these outstanding
bills. We could have applied to the town council and borrowed the money from the town contingency fund, but
if we did that, someone on that council would inevitably
order us to turn over any money we made from using
the copy machine, and put it in the general fund. Nah,
bad idea, I thought. We used the receipts from the copy
machine to buy flowers for sick family members, new
babies, funerals and other incidentals. Consequently,
the borrowed Jeep fund money paid off the outstanding bills. The borrowed money amounted to less than
five hundred dollars. The loan was paid back, but not to
the Jeep fund. Over a short amount of time every cent
of borrowed money was paid back, but it was transferred
to an interest bearing account. We didn't think it was
necessary to tell anyone in authority in the town what
we had done. We just told the town council president,

Stanley Jendzejec, and told him where the money was. He just blew it off and said,

"That's good."

Remember the misappropriation of funds leveled at me before the grand jury? The grand jury was given the idea that I was pilfering the fund for own personal use. I suppose the attorney general's investigators could see that I was living in the lap of luxury; new car, expensive clothes, etc. Needless to say that notion never went anywhere but the seed was planted. Sometimes that's enough.

Those nice ladies and gentlemen were investigating our Jeep fund based on the recommendation of someone (I wonder who?), and went to see the attorney general of the state. There was never any question in my mind who suggested they complain to the attorney general.

The attorney general, Richard Isreal, jumped all over the situation and made it a separate investigation when he was tearing the entire department apart. He even accused me of "possibly" embezzling the money or misusing it in some other manner. You see, this worm didn't have to prove anything. All he had to do was plant the seed in the grand jury's mind and I would have to defend our actions and prove we had done nothing wrong. Attorney general Isreal subpoenaed the president of the Coventry Credit Union to testify before the grand jury regarding where the police department fund money was? The attorney general never asked if the money was in an interest bearing account or if we were getting interest on the taxpayer's private donations. The attorneys general wanted to paint the picture that there was money there in a financial institution, but there was a period of time when some money was missing.

Hellooo, the money was never missing, you goof. It was transferred to another account, and paid back with interest. The town council president knew it, but he was never called to testify.

If ever there needed to be an investigation, federal authorities should have investigated the attorney general's office. Who would ask for something like that? Isreal is the man that should have been removed from office for abusing his authority and violating the obligations and duties of his office.

By the way, the remainder of the Jeep fund was used to purchase a police patrol boat for the same people who populated the lake areas previously described. We put a stop to the crazy boat racers and other questionable water practices in one summer. From information I gathered, the feed-back was all favorable and the Jeep incident forgotten. I recently heard that the police boat still runs nearly forty years later.

CHAPTER 20

While on the state police, all of our patrol troopers would perform a specific function for the local school district. If we had a grade school in the area, someone in the patrol division would stand a school patrol twice a day; morning and afternoon. The troopers weren't crazy about squiring little kids across an intersection, when it could easily have been done by the local cops. Finally, Colonel Walter Stone became superintendant of state police and ended that little pain in the bucket detail. All school districts had crossing guards and if they could get out of it without having the taxpayer front the cost for crossing guards, they would prevail on the state police.

Coventry had their own crossing guards, eighteen of them. These women were spread out all over the town. Some as far away as twelve miles in very rural areas, but most of them were within the more congested districts. The crossing guards had a makeshift uniform and looked fairly presentable. They wore a white blouse, dark knee length skirt and a navy blue jacket. Their heads were covered with a white hat looking much like a navy wave's hat. They also wore reflective crossing belts and all had a whistle. I heard some of the women complaining that motorists, many times, would drive right through their stop order while they were trying to help the children cross safely. These women had to stay alert having only a minimal amount of training with moving vehicles.

I asked Lieutenant Andy Wallace if he thought it would be a good idea to have these ladies sworn in as special police officers. We would give them authority to stop a flagrant violator and refer that motorist to the police department for further action if it were warranted. Simply, we would put some teeth in the crossing guard operation. They would no longer be referred to as crossing guards but as special police officers. Andy thought it was a great idea. Then I dropped the bomb on him.

"Andy," I said, "You are going to be their training officer and teach them what they need to know about traffic and handling children and adults in a professional manner. We will start a media blitz and make sure the public gets the word." Andy enthusiastically agreed and would get started immediately. I told him he would have unrestricted access to anything the department had that might help, including an assistant.

Lieutenant Wallace got together with several of the women and redesigned their uniforms. The uniforms made them look more like regular members of the department, up to and including the Stetson hats.

From its inception, the project was a complete success. The women all worked together, held their own meetings to discuss their type of work, and made a tremendous contribution. In the years I remained as police chief, I never heard of a problem involving the special police women.

As you might imagine, the rumors began immediately. The ladies police organization was dubbed, "Harvey's Harem."

Andy was fooling around with a female member and his marriage was in jeopardy. Several other women were "absolutely" seen going in and coming out of motels with men.

None of this was true, but it became fodder for the local gossip mill. Welcome to living and working in Coventry, Rhode Island.

CHAPTER 21

It was early into my tenure and, as usual, attendance at the regular town council meeting was mandatory. During the meeting, one of my police officers came rushing into the council chambers and whispered that we had a bad situation in town. The officer hurriedly went on to tell me that a man had gone berserk at the western end of town and was holding his wife and children at bay with a shot gun, threatening to kill them.

I excused myself, quickly exited the council chambers with the police officer, and ordered every available police cruiser to the area. I also had our dispatcher tell them not to move until I got there. If anyone was going to make the wrong decision, it was going to be me.

We arrived in approximately twelve minutes. The man in question owned and operated a small country gas station and lived in the house several yards away. There were no convenience marts in those days. Behind the station itself, there was a two car garage housing an old pick-up truck. Auto parts from vehicles that had been worked on were lying around here and there. I could not see a weapon in his hand, but I had been warned there was a rifle lying on the seat of the truck. I decided to greet the situation head-on.

I walked in on the wide dirt and gravel driveway. The man was easily visible. My orders were that everyone was to stay out of sight and out of the line of fire, if he did decide to shoot. I would handle this and they were to back me up. I didn't do it to be a hero, it's just the way I was trained. I was confident I could resolve this matter.

My approach toward the man was careful, and I was ready to dive out of the way to either side of the driveway if I had to. I was slowly and cautiously getting closer. I was familiar with this person and knew he was a "bad dude" when he was drinking. I noticed a couple of empty beer bottles on the truck hood so apparently he had been drinking.

I shouted his name, "Webster, I want to talk to you. This is Chief Simmons."

The man never moved.

He was wearing a dark blue work shirt with the sleeves rolled up and matching trousers; mechanics clothes. His hair was dark and wavy, and he had a good sturdy build for his six foot tall frame. His weight was between two hundred ten to two hundred twenty pounds. He looked like he could have been an athlete. The thought flashed through my mind that he was about two inches taller than me and had me by twenty pounds. Could I take him down? We'll see.

I walked up a little closer. Webster still had not moved.

Suddenly he sprang like a cat to the door of the truck.

Everyone outside stood up.

"Stay back," I ordered in a loud but calm voice.

About fifteen police officers squatted back down. I was thinking where the hell did we get all this help?

"Webster, hold it," I said. "If you come out of that truck window with a weapon in your hand, you're a dead man." With that, I pulled my snub-nose colt thirty eight out of my waist holster. I did not point the revolver at him. I knew I had the drop on him and just kept the gun pointing at the ground.

Webster just looked at me. We were within ten feet of one another. If he grabbed the shotgun out of the truck, I knew I had better make the first shot count because I would be no match for a twelve gauge shotgun. My reasoning said he wouldn't miss at this range, and not if the gun was loaded with buckshot. We discovered later that it was a twelve gauge, and it was loaded with extra strength buckshot, enough to bring down a large animal, and easily a one hundred eighty five pound police chief.

"Stop right there," Webster growled. "This is my property."

I responded with, "Not when we get a complaint from another member of this household it's not," as I continued approaching him very slowly.

Ever stand face to face with an irrational, unhinged person? I looked into his eyes and saw the rage and rebellion hidden deep in his senses. Oh shit, I thought, this isn't going to end well.

"Hold it," he bellowed again. Webster grabbed his young son by the shoulder. The boy was no more than ten or eleven years old, and it was obvious he was terrified. The lad had been standing nearby all this time. Concern for this boy was another reason why I did not point my gun at the father, or let my officers anywhere near the scene.

"What the hell kind of man are you?" I asked, "Hiding behind a small boy."

I was hoping this statement would make the father mad and he would shove the boy out of the way and come at me to show how tough he was. It worked! He threw the boy aside, and glared at me. He made a move to reach through the truck window diverting his attention from me for a second. That was all I needed, and I dove at him across a distance of probably five feet. I hit him with a flying tackle right around the chest and we both tumbled to the ground. Fortunately, I landed on top of him. I threw my gun back out toward the driveway in the event I lost this battle. I didn't want that handgun within Webster's reach. My police officers were charging in like the cavalry, and the situation was over in a few seconds. My guys had Webster restrained, and in a police cruiser headed to jail.

His terrified wife grabbed up the boy as I approached both of them, promising nothing bad was going to happen to her husband at the police station. There would be a number of charges brought against him and he would be arraigned the following morning in our local district court. I told her she could drop some clean clothes off at the station so he might look a little more presentable before the judge. She agreed to do so.

There was a law that allows a person to withdraw charges against an alleged violator. It was passed some years back due to the fact that many domestic violence complaints were withdrawn after an overnight of thinking and, "he won't do it anymore". You would be surprised how many times charges were withdrawn and the police officers then looked like the bad guys. You would also probably be surprised at how many times the wives regretted their decisions because, inevitably, it happened again.

A policy was instituted, supported by the courts that required a complainant to post a fifty dollar surety bond before the abuser would be charged and arraigned in court. That was not the case here. I did not ask the wife for bond money and we went ahead and charged him.

Yup, you guessed it! Daylight brought remorse, Mrs. Webster refused to testify, and the court had to dismiss the case. That was an all too familiar pattern, but I can't really blame her. She has to live with this jerk. I wondered if she realized the possible consequences that went with her decision.

Fortunately, I never heard from either of them again.

Certainly, not realizing it at the time, I was to learn through the grapevine, the incident inspired a great deal of respect from members of my department. Allegedly, it was said, the chief really "has guts". Imagine if I had guessed wrong? My "guts" could easily have been splattered all over that country driveway on a fall evening in 1969.

Thanks for the backup guys.

CHAPTER 22

April 1970 got us closer to election time. I received a call from Al Frechette, the town solicitor, who liked to remind me how he used his broad scope of power to get me appointed chief of police. He was about to do it again, remind me, that is. I didn't think the ruling party would have a problem getting re-elected. They didn't.

Just as a short side story.

It was February and there was a primary election in town. During the year I had been chief, I professed my "non-political" affiliation to any party. I was not a politician and did not want to create any perception of being beholden to one party or another.

I was at my mother's house, the phone rang and it was Stanley. My step-father answered and as directed, he told Stanley I was not there. I warned my step-father that I was being hunted to go to vote in the democratic primary and I did not want to do that. Literally, I asked him to lie for me. He did, but Stanley badgered him and said they really needed my vote. Pop hung up.

He said to me, "I'll be right back."

It was a rainy miserable night and Pop was not feeling well at all, but he backed out of the yard and was back home in twenty minutes. I asked what he did. He told me he went to the voting place and voted for the "party" and then went up to Stanley and said, "There is the Chief's vote." You think I had a pair of large gonads?

The political bosses were not happy because their police chief did not show up at the primary. Truly, what pissed me off was they were all going back on their "absolute" promises not to involve me in their political party. Now I was learning the hard way that politicians are literally full of shit. The attitude of, "We want what's good for us and we don't care about anyone else" was becoming more and more apparent to me.

I received another call from Al Frechette who told me he wanted me to fix a speeding ticket for a friend.

"Al," I replied, "you know I won't fix a speeding ticket. That will just demoralize the men." Fixing tickets is a part of our culture and it has been going on for as long as tickets have been issued. It had to stop. Everyone who has been stopped and ticketed legally goes to court. Here it comes!

"Look," Al bellowed, I helped you get this job, what did I do, create a monster?"

"Al, if that's the way you want to look at it, you're entitled, but I still won't fix a traffic ticket. I thought I was on pretty solid ground by now, so what could I lose for not fixing a ticket? What an expensive lesson I was to learn.

Frechette ranted over the telephone. Finally, I heard enough and quietly hung up. He called back and said,

"Remember, big shot we control your budget."

"Stick it up your ass," was my reply and I hung up again. I was upset because of the way he was pressuring me lately anyway.

By the way, the ticket the town solicitor wanted fixed was due to one of my patrol officers chasing a vehicle through a crowded bathing beach reaching speeds of 90 MPH in an area zoned at 15 MPH. We didn't do much drunk driver testing in those days, so this guy was given a ride home and just charged with speeding. Frechette didn't want to hear it because this person was allegedly a big contributor to the Democratic party. Keep in mind, Frechette is the chief law enforcement officer in the town, just like the attorney general is to the state.

In March 1970, I learned he hadn't forgotten. At the budget hearings, all department heads had to present a budget request for finances for the upcoming year. The council is responsible for approving, increasing or cutting those submissions. At the hearing, it was time for the police department budget, and I arose from my seat to make my presentation of our budget. Everything had all been approved a week prior to this meeting behind closed doors, so this was nothing more than a formality. As I stood Stanley lightly tugged at my sport coat and said,

"Sit down and relax, I'll take it from here."

I didn't say anything, just sat back down.

Stanley recited the line by line budget items from salaries to equipment requested by the police department. The final total turned out to be $40,000 less than we agreed upon at our closed budget meeting a week earlier. I sat there among about 250 people stupefied. I felt this weak little tap on my shoulder. When I looked back over my shoulder, I saw that it was Frechette seated directly behind me.

He leaned forward and stuck his hawk nosed, be-speckled , pointy face at me and said, "The next time we ask for a ticket to be fixed you'll probably want to do it".

I wanted to twist further around in the seat and belt him upside the head, but I held steady.

One sunny summer afternoon, after my expensive go-round with Frechette, his democratic pal made another attempt at a speed run through the bathing beach, and struck and killed a teenage boy who was attempting to cross the roadway from a frozen lemonade stand.

I called Frechette seething with anger, "Hey Al, you want to fix this one?" He hung up on me.

Regardless of how the pie is cut, the politicians will nail you one way or another. I don't give a damn where it is, or at what level, the mighty hand of politics is into everything and amazingly there are many palms to grease. Everyone is looking for a handout; even my little friend Frechette, and also Stanley Jendzejec, who was an ice cream salesman, living in a very prominent section of town very near a popular lake. Go figure. I don't mean to say all politicians are dishonest, just the majority. It is really easy to tell an honest politician; he or she doesn't usually have much, and don't last very long unless they cave. Politics is kind of like big business gobbling up smaller businesses. You either join or get crushed. I never joined the group. You can work out the rest. In any event, Frechette was about to get a little payback. Justice can be swift.

CHAPTER 23

I was sitting in my office one morning, when the telephone rang. The caller was a member of the Rhode Island Division of Law Enforcement. States have various names for what these people do. In Rhode Island, this department used to be called the Department of Fish and Game. The officers patrolled state parks and beaches. The caller asked to speak with me and identified himself as Charlie Barwell, whom I had known for a number of years, going back to my state police patrol days.

The call started pleasant enough. Charlie and I did a little reminiscing over the nights he would come by Hope Valley barracks, up near the Connecticut state line and ask if he could ride with me for part of the evening. I, of course, welcomed the company. Charlie was a really nice guy. He asked if we could meet sometime during the afternoon that day. He said he had something he would like to talk to me about, but it shouldn't be discussed over the telephone. What now? I wondered.

At 3: 30 that afternoon Charlie Barwell came into my office with a folder full of papers. He dropped several investigative cases on my desk and kindly asked me to open them and read. I did.

After a moment, I looked at Officer Barwell and mumbled, "Holy shit!" I couldn't believe what I read.

Charlie gave me this forlorn look and said, "It's true, I was the one that got him."

It seems our little friend, Albert Frechette, visited a small rest area in a neighboring town. Barwell pulled into the roadside park and noticed a man sitting in a car alone. The guy in the car gave an admiring glance, nodded his head and licked his lips. Frechette got out of his car and entered one side of a double outdoor privy, (outhouse). Barwell got out of his car and entered the other side. According to the report, there was a hole in the partition just below what would be an average man's waistline. As the story goes, the object is to insert a penis through the hole and the man on the other side would enjoy a little homosexual treat. As it turned out, of course, the man on the other side of the wall was a member of the Rhode Island Division of Law Enforcement. While Frechette had his penis in the hole, Barwell exited the other booth and entered Frechette's, identified himself as a law enforcement officer and made the arrest. Frechette was told the department would be contacting him and would issue a warrant to appear in open court on a charge of being lewd and lascivious and disorderly conduct.

Instead of handling this incident in the normal manner, Charlie Barwell returned to his office and presented his arrest information to his boss, Mr. John Rego who was the director of the division. Thank God for Johnny Rego.

Mr. Rego informed officer Barwell that the young police chief in Coventry had had enough tragedy to deal with recently, and didn't need more problems heaped on his shoulders. John Rego suggested Charlie come to me, and lay it at my feet. Charlie advised me that I could handle it however I wanted, as long as Frechette was removed from office and sent on his way. Otherwise, his department would have to charge Frechette publicly.

Certainly I knew Al Frechette was married, had two very young daughters, owned a reasonably nice, older home, and was on the rise in the political ranks. I didn't want to see him or anyone else get taken down publicly, so I was given a choice. I did have an opportunity to keep a lid on this thing and not embarrass the town further. Charlie suggested I inform the town council president, Stanley Jendzejec, and let him deal with it. I did! There were things I didn't know.

Shortly thereafter I came to work one morning to learn Al Frechette, his wife and children were gone. It was as though they had vanished. I was informed that Frechette had taken his family to Las Vegas to resume his law career there.

Attorney Frechette had a young law partner named Arthur G. Capaldi. Capaldi had been out of law school about a year and now he was in line to become the Coventry town solicitor. Arthur and I became pretty good friends, or at least I thought we were. Politics can do strange things to people. Arthur told me one day that when Al cleaned out his office he remarked to him that "someday everyone will know the truth". Neither of us knew what that might have meant, but I was to find out....!

For those of us that know the ways of a small New England town, it didn't take long for rumors to circulate regarding why Albert Frechette made such a hasty retreat from the state. The fascinating things were the reports heard from people who were totally disassociated with town happenings, and really knew nothing about what went on. The rumor mongers knew much more about the incident and circumstances than any of us who were directly involved. It was almost uncanny to learn peoples' thoughts because they appeared to have nothing better to do than cast stones at someone else. This is obviously a way of life, and not just in Coventry, Rhode Island. It's everywhere. As much as I hated rumors and malicious stories, I even found myself caught up in this web of destructive gossip from time to time.

After I turned over Officer Barwell's reports to Stanley he arranged for a meeting with persons unknown to me, although I could take a guess. Frechette was confronted and given a choice. "Get out of town or I'll blow the whistle on you." Some choice!

The months and years to come were to enlighten me much more!

It seems that Al Frechette was Stanley's campaign manager when he was running for town council. Stanley made it obvious, after he was elected, that he was the local political ruler and no longer needed Frechette's ambition or assistance. He now had the golden opportunity to get rid of him. Although I hate to belabor the point, it is amazing to me how low and rotten local politics can get. You can find it everywhere.

The state Police Chief's Association had a meeting monthly, (party if you will) in a different part of the state, and it was my turn to host this affair. My guest speaker was a US congressman named Paul Baird who was not a regular member of the establishment. That means he lasted two years, and got trounced because he would not get involved in the dirty game of politics. He used to carry small paint brushes with him and hand them out saying he was going to make a clean sweep of dirty politics. Two years later, the party came up with a "player" and Baird was gone. While we were sitting at the head table I leaned over and asked him what politics was like in Washington. He told me everyone, on both sides of the aisle, pretty much got along. The viciousness in politics was at the lower level. The fight was to get through local politics, progress to the state level, and then on to a national office, if you could get an endorsement. I never forgot his statement, "The worst politics and backstabbing is on the local level".

No one cares what happens to a guy like Frechette, just as long as they can ruin him, embarrass him, and if it affects his family and friends, so what? They need to destroy his life and bring him down in total disgrace.

Trust me, I know. The throat cutting usually takes place within the same party, and little or nothing is done to ward off the onslaught of the opposition. You can't fight what you can't see. I didn't have a party and was trying to remain neutral. It became obvious that was not going to happen.

I attended council meeting after council meeting, and listened to the heated exchanges. Time and again I thought they would come to blows, but it seemed there was an unwritten rule. Stanley Jendzejec would prevail. He always got his way. He could lie, cheat or steal, but no one dared defy him, or attempt to gain support from any other group opposing the good ole boys.

Within the Democratic party, I learned there were cliques that would attempt to undermine issues that were being pushed by the town council. As I previously explained, the Democratic town committee usually made recommendations to the town council concerning appointments to the police and highway departments and other town employees. It was always Stanley that emerged victorious when an issue needed to be settled. Not only was he the president of the town council, he was also the chairman of the Democratic town committee. Stan told me one day that the council president was nothing more than a figure head. The real power and authority was the chairman of the party. He was to be stripped of all that power and have his political future ruined one day, but before he crashed and burned, he took a few people with him. I was one of them.

CHAPTER 24

At a police committee meeting one evening, a councilman began a discussion about fixing tickets. Remember those political considerations? I explained once again, I wasn't in favor of fixing tickets, all of the councilmen knew that from the beginning of my administration as police chief. The councilman told me he didn't particularly care what I was in favor of. I worked for the Town of Coventry town council and I had better do what I was told or I could find myself in deep trouble. As I recall, I told him to go to hell in no uncertain terms. I could understand the committee and the town council recommending changes that would benefit the department and the public; changes that would benefit the department, not damage it. I would have no difficulty with change even if it was against my better judgment. I wasn't the end all, be all and I encouraged suggestions from everyone, but I would not change the "no fix" traffic ticket policy. I wasn't going to change my approach to pacify them, or more specifically one man, Eddie Jacques. He was always there, wasn't he, like a boil on the ass.

I refused to allow these men to use the police department as their personal play toy just to gain votes. The argument got more heated and I had had enough. I got up from my chair and made some really dumb-ass remark like "I will arrest the whole goddamned bunch of you for interfering with the operation of this police department and the duty of a police officer before you fire me." I wasn't being too stupid. The councilmen kept yelling and making threats as I walked out of the room. When I cooled down, I usually called or visited with whichever councilman I had offended and apologized. Eddie Jacques was never gracious enough to accept an apology. He was a treacherous and vindictive bastard. That opinion was shared by more than just me. Jacques could keep that smirky little grin on his face while he was twisting the knife in your back.

It has been said that it was easier to fire a police chief than to fire a police officer. Who would have believed that? It was true. The lower ranks of police officers had union representation that protected their members, whereas the chief of police had no protection at all. A police chief in New Haven, Connecticut was fired, and asked for support from a local union and was refused. He couldn't go to the city for financial and legal assistance because they were the ones that fired him. He was left swinging in the breeze. Most police chiefs I knew did not make a lot of money and couldn't afford good legal representation. End result; not many chiefs kept their jobs, and built up big legal fees anyway. I know I did.

In 1972 I attended a Rhode Island Police Chiefs meeting after I had been suspended. I addressed the assembly and asked for their support, and band behind me and perhaps offer some legal assistance so that I could fight back. I reminded them if the Coventry town council were allowed to do this unrestricted or unopposed, it would open the door for other cities in the state to have open season on their police chiefs because we had no support system. My comments were met with mild applause and a few uttered remarks of "Good luck" and that was about it. I felt like my comments fell on deaf ears. Twenty-six fired police chiefs later, they were to find out I was right. That's correct. Within the next two years twenty-six other police chiefs were outright fired because they knew Coventry got away with firing me. Like me, all had permanent status. There is always someone else that wants that job and will do whatever it takes to get it, even if it means becoming a Victor Pajak and turning on you. Later I will go into more detail about the council wanting to fire Pajak on two occasions and I went to bat for him both publicly and with the councilmen. I even got his suspension lifted. He, on the other hand, never lifted a finger to help me and even swore out a phony arrest warrant against me that was later thrown out and dismissed. In fairness to Pajak, I learned he, along with others, was intimidated into this by the attorney general.

Why then would anyone give up a relatively good job to accept this kind of responsibility? Why did I? I had a really decent position as a state police detective and in nine more years I would have been eligible for a retirement with a pension. I was warned, but obviously didn't listen. Was it prestige, power, glory, recognition, connections or even the opportunity to accept or take graft (be in the take)?

The answer would be a loud resounding NO!

None of those reasons! I recall the time the little girl in my neighborhood had her arm badly damaged in the lawn mower accident and the smart remarks and wise-cracks about the Coventry police arriving at the scene. I didn't know at that time that I would have an opportunity to become the police chief, and stop the jokes and slanderous remarks, and give the police department the respect and leadership it should have had. I loved my town. I grew up with these people, and I was determined to give them what they deserved, the best we had to offer. I felt I had done that, but politically, I obviously didn't please everyone.

Graft, corruption and political favors? Did these temptations prevail in a police chief's life. Yes! I certainly know how much I was paid. I took a pay cut to accept the job and was going to work more years toward retirement than I would have as a state trooper. I knew what most police chief's salary ranges were and they weren't going to live in expensive homes or drive really nice personal vehicles or even send their kids to an Ivy league college. I didn't even give these things much consideration since I grew up relatively poor, the son of a very hardworking woman. We didn't have much, but what we did have was through honest hard work. I felt the same as the chief.

One day I was in attendance at a police chief's function but I was not yet a member of the police chief's association. Another chief was urging me to become a member so the association would have 100 percent participation. I was told by this chief, who worked in the neighboring town, that I should make friends and "glad hand" the businessmen and do a favor or two. I said,

"Bill, I don't operate that way and I would hate to think I owed someone."

"Oh, you need to go along to get along," he repeated.

I just nodded, excused myself and walked away.

I did join the association but never became an active participant. Almost immediately after I was fired, the same police chief was fired. Guess he didn't go along well enough.

Nice homes, cars and swimming pools. When I was fired I had no home, no car, certainly no back yard to put a swimming pool in and eight dollars to my name. Guess I wasn't in the game long enough, or know the right people. I didn't care to hang out with the leaches and hangers on or other less notables, I didn't care much for those who bought the testimonial tickets by the bunch. I would attend a testimonial or other formal affair and be asked to sit at the head table with other well known people. I never saw myself as that important and there were many men in attendance that were more deserving than me. Friends? They were plentiful. When the tables turned they became very hard to find.

I walked into functions for a social evening with a friend or two and was greeted by people that just wanted to either be seen with you, shake your hand, brush off your clothes with a whisk broom or dust off your shoes.

There were times when I would pick up a phone and call someone requesting what could have been inter-preted as a small favor. The reaction was unbelievable. I would hear responses like "You bet my friend," "You just ask, it yours," Is that all you need," How about a lit-tle something for you chief?" It went on. One day a local businessman walked into my office and tossed a couple of tickets on my desk.

"What are those," I asked? The man owned a liquor store.

He said they were for a testimonial dinner for someone. I don't remember who.

I asked bluntly why he was giving the tickets to me.

"Oh, that's OK, I used to do it all the time for the old chief." The liquor store owner replied.

"Well, I am afraid I can't accept them," I said. "If I decide to go, I'll buy my own ticket."

"Oh no", the man said, "it's perfectly alright, everyone does this."

Perhaps he was right, it did go on all of the time, but I wasn't about to sell my department out for a couple of tickets to a testimonial, and especially for a party I wasn't crazy about going to anyway.

I finally said, "Look, you give these tickets to someone else if you want to, but I can't accept them and will not take them."

"Thank you for your kind thoughts," I finally said, and returned to the task at hand. He got the message and left with the tickets in hand. We never became good friends.

The incident had nothing to do with testimonial tickets, but less than a week later, I received information that the same liquor store owner was rumored to be selling liquor to minors. I never got enough information to make an arrest, but, I did start an investigation. Imagine, if I had accepted the tickets?

Some information was passed along to me from one of my detectives that one of my senior officers called the liquor store owner and told him to watch out because I was out to get him. Although it was damn near criminal to inform suspects that they are being watched by the police department. I never did find out who the "fink" (informer) was, but it did serve a purpose. The under-age drinking complaints stopped.

CHAPTER 25

Early in 1970 I registered at a local college, and began taking law enforcement courses. Specifically, to enhance my management knowledge. Bryant College was a small business college in Providence, with a campus in the city of Warwick, Rhode Island. Several other members of the Coventry police department also enrolled. The federal government footed the bill for this education under a bill sponsored by President Nixon. It was a win-win situation for police officers all over the state and in Massachusetts as well.

One evening, after classes, Victor Pajak, a lieutenant at the time, and I dropped off a fellow student who was a detective from the city of Warwick. On the way home the lieutenant started to unfold a tale that set me back on my heels. Lieutenant Pajak was a rather large man of polish extraction with a big round head and looked like a Scandanavian. I had known Vic ever since I was a teenager. We all viewed Vic Pajak as a jokester who's most important role in life was cracking those non- funny Italian jokes. I never told him about the ton of Polish jokes that floated around constantly. Say what you will though, Pajak lasted twenty four years. I had an administration that last three years. He must have done something right but I don't want to get into Pajak's career moves right here.

"You know, chief," Vic Pajak began, "I was talking to that detective from Warwick PD and you know what he told me about our friend Stanley?"

"Stanley who", I asked?

"Jendzejec our esteemed town council president."

"What about him", I inquired?

Lieutenant Pajak went on to say that a couple of nights ago Stanley got picked up in a rest area in Attleboro, Massachusetts.

"For what," I asked?

Victor blurted out very emphatically, "For trying to stick it up some kids dirt shoot."

"**What!**" My mind said no, not Stanley.

"Ya, no shit," Vic went on, "And you want to know the best part?"

"Not really" I answered, "But I'm sure you're going to tell me."

"The kid Stanley was going to sock it to was colored."

"Oh bullshit," I almost yelled.

"No honest," Pajak pleaded. "The two Attleboro cops go to school at Bryant, and they told a couple of guys from Warwick PD, and they told me."

"Are these guys still on campus, I asked?"

"No but they have classes on Wednesday night like we do."

"I'd like to speak with one of them," I said. "Until I do, you are not to say a damned word to anyone." I thought about how ridiculous that statement was. Telephone, telegraph, tell-a-Vic. The world will know within hours.

The following Wednesday when we returned to college, my mind was not on class. I went to the first class and as soon as it was over, Pajak and I met with one of the two Attleboro, Mass. police officers. We met at the college canteen. The Massachusetts cop was there right on time.

The Attleboro officer told us he and his partner work from midnight to eight in the morning, sometimes. At other times they work a staggered shift; something like nine o'clock at night until five o'clock in the morning. This particular night they were working a staggered shift. They pulled their police cruiser into a rest area off Route I-95. The park was just over the Rhode Island/Massachusetts state line in Attleboro. The officers observed a late model blue Chevrolet with the windows all fogged up. The police officer, telling me the story, said he approached the driver's side of the car, looked in to see a fairly large man remove his hands from a colored males hips, sit upright in the car and hastily zip up his trousers. The police officer asked the man what he was doing there and the big man said they just stopped to talk and were just leaving. The Attleboro officer did obtain identification from the driver and the black male. The driver was identified as Stanley M. Jendzejec of 12 Appleblosson Lane in Coventry, R. I. The youth was identified as Ernest Carr of Wadsworth St. Providence, Rhode Iasland.

I asked the police officer what he thought Stanley was doing or about to do?

"Jesus Christ chief, I didn't see that much but he didn't leave any doubt in my mind that he was going to screw this kid in the ass."

"What did Mr. Jendzejec say to you," I asked the officer?

"He showed me a green identification card and told me he was the Coventry police commissioner."

The officer went on to say that he told the pair they should probably move on **NOW** and made that pretty emphatic, and he didn't want to see them in this area again. Jendzejec nodded and drove off.

I thanked the officer, we shook hands and we parted.

To say I was dumbfounded is putting it mildly, I never had any suspicion that Stanley Jendzejec was a switch hitter. He was married with two sons. I wondered how in the hell a man gets like that? How does a man like Stanley have an appetite for other men.

Now, I began putting the pieces of the puzzle together. I could pretty well figure out why Stanley wanted to get rid of Al Frechette. Jendzejec knew Albert Frechette was queer and Al Frechette also knew Stanley was gay or bi-sexual. Stanley was really pissed that Al got caught in a rest area with another man that turned out to be an officer of the Department of Law Enforcement. Aside from any embarrassment Al Frechette may have caused the town of Coventry, Stanley had to have been pissed that his lover cheated on him. Can any of this be proven? Speculation maybe, but I have grave doubts that either of them would take a lie detector (polygraph) test. What a stinking mess.

Again, I called Art Capaldi. Seems like Art and I were always in the middle of some outlandish, jumbled up pile of human waste. We decided to go visit the undisputed leader of the town, Senator Wiliam Fecteau. Old Bill was liked and admired by just about everyone, including me. Bill ran a small insurance agency in town, and was in the state general assembly for twelve years. It was obvious he devoted his spare time to politics. He was a politician's politician. I called him "Gov."

I explained the story about Stanley as Lieutenant Pajak and I heard it from the Attleboro police officer. He was as flabbergasted as anyone. Senator Fecteau was grooming Stanley to replace him in the state senate just as he had guided Stanley up through local politics.

"Holy Christ," the senator said, "That stupid son of a bitch. If this is true, we are going to have to do something. We don't want and can't afford another Frechette mess."

I asked what he thought I should do, if anything?

"Does Stanley know about this yet," the senator asked?

"No," I replied.

"Are you going to tell him," the senator asked?

"I haven't given that much thought", I answered.

The senator suggested, "Why don't you, and see what his reaction is?"

Why me I thought? Why am I always the one. Goddamn it my brain screamed.

I was mad. Mad at Stanley, mad at Frechette, mad at the guys that got me involved in the murder and just plain mad in general. This invisible little guy was yelling in my ear, "This shit has to end sometime, doesn't it?"

I drove Art Capaldi back to his office. We had little to say to one another. I went back to my office.

Stanley stopped by the town hall every day and usually visited my office. It was like sitting on razor blades waiting and wondering what to do or say to him.

As anticipated, Stanley came into the office at 3:30 that afternoon. It was April 1970 and the weather was just starting to break from a long cold winter, and not too pleasant a spring so far. Maybe that was an omen.

"Stan, you got a few minutes," I asked?

"Sure," he said in his normal gentlemanly manner. Only a few times did I ever see him get upset because of the weight of office, his family or his full time job. He was an ice cream salesman for a large dairy company in Providence. Stanley was under a lot of pressure and stress, but yet he always handled himself gracefully. However, this was to change as he added more and more power to his personal empire.

"Let's take a ride," I said.

Stan agreed, we got into my car, and I began to unfold the story.

"Stanley, last week Vic Pajak told me a story he heard third hand from a Warwick PD detective, who allegedly heard it from an Attleboro, Massachusetts police officer."

"What was that," Stanley asked?

"Have you ever been stopped and checked out by the Attleboro, Mass, police department?"

"No not that I can remember."

"Well, you better think hard," I prompted. "Do you recall being in a rest area just off Interstate 95 a couple of weeks ago, and you had a colored kid in the car with you?"

Stanley turned white, as all of the color drained from his face.

"Why, what are you talking about," Stanley hurriedly asked?

"Look Stan, I don't know what the hell happened but you were there. Maybe you are being set up by someone or someone paid off the Attleboro cop. I don't know, I wasn't there, but you know what happened." He was purposely avoiding my glances.

"Jesus" he said, "what am I going to do?" His inquiry was more of a plea than a question. He was obviously looking for help.

"About the only thing I can suggest is that I go to Attleboro and follow up on this and see if I can find out if the Attleboro police officer kept any reports." Stan, they have your name and address and the black kids name and address. I was unbelieving too so I spoke with Art Capaldi and Senator Fecteau about it. Carl Brown, one of my detectives, knows about it, as does Vic Pajak. You know damned well if Pajak knows, everyone at the Brookside Inn (a local bar and eatery) will know, if they don't already.

"What did the senator say," Stanley asked?

"He thinks Capaldi and I and Carl Brown should follow up."

Still visibly shaking, Stan restated, "What the hell am I going to do?"

"We need to call Capaldi and see what we can do."

I called Art Capaldi, the town solicitor, and he was at my office in a matter of minutes. We talked for hours and the council president never once broke or admitted anything, nor did I expect him to.

Arthur Capaldi finally stated he thought we should all go to Attleboro, find the two cops and see if they could make a positive identification. Stan began to stutter and stammer.

"Jesus," he said, "I don't know. I haven't been home for supper and my wife will be worried. I haven't spent much time with her lately and I should be home with her."

Any doubt we might have had was quickly vanishing as both Art and I felt he was hiding the truth.

I located Detective Carl Brown, a short rugged rebel from Alabama who did a stint in the Navy at Quonset Point Naval air station in North Kingston, Rhode Island. He met his wife in Rhode Island and ended up staying there. Carl was a former part time police officer in the neighboring town of West Warwick. Over a period of several years, I had come to know Carl and had occasion to work with him when I was a state police detective. He knew his stuff and was a good, hardworking investigator. He wanted to come to Coventry and work with our department. Tom Jones was probably the only other member of the police department that I felt was as dedicated as Carl Brown. I did a little battling with the local politicians to get Carl on board because he lived in the adjacent town and was not a Coventry resident. Qualifications meant nothing. Carl made some promises he never intended to keep. I looked the other way and Carl did become a member of our department. He never did move to Coventry. A little over a year with the department, and I made him a detective. I never regretted that decision.

Carl Brown, Art Capaldi and I left for Attleboro. Stanley went home. It was after midnight when the three of us arrived in the small western Massachusetts town. We went to the police station and I introduced myself to the desk lieutenant, a man well over six feet tall and probably 250 pounds. Typical Irish cop, I thought.

I asked if we could possibly talk with a couple of his men concerning an incident that may have happened in his jurisdiction involving an official of the town of Coventry. I told him the names of the two police officers. Fortunately both were on duty and out on patrol. The officers were summoned and came into the station immediately. We went into the chief's office. We explained why we were there and showed them a couple of photographs and asked if they could pick out the man they interviewed that night in the rest area. One officer couldn't pick Stanley out of a photograph recently taken at a testimonial dinner. They were shown another picture of Stanley standing over my shoulder. The picture was out of a local newspaper article. After a moment, the police officer pointed at me in the picture and said "that looks like him". Really sharp cop, I thought. I was standing right in front of him and he couldn't make the distinction. Capaldi, Brown and I looked at one another and winced. We thanked the two police officers and left. That evening had fizzled.

On our way back to Coventry none of us were absolutely certain that it was Stanley in the car with the black kid. Maybe it was because we didn't want to believe it. What I was sure of, was that we had enough trouble for now.

It was about two forty-five in the morning when we stopped at Stanley's house to let him know what had transpired. We all had a good laugh and went home to bed. I'll bet Stanley gave a huge sigh, "whew" that's over. Not yet Mr. President, not yet.

To complete the investigation, I knew we had to find Ernest Carr in Providence. Detective Brown and I hunted all over the city of Providence. Providence was what we ran into. We stopped to briefly talk with a young black boy walking on the street and asked if he knew Ernest Carr. The lad was about five or six years old and blurted out immediately, "Sure, that my uncle". We asked where Uncle Ernest lived feeling exalted for doing such fine police work. Police investigators constantly tell you they have good informants or "snitches" that keep them in the loop. That's a lot of crap. Most of the time, it is pure luck, and that is exactly what our encounter with Carr's nephew was.

My uncle lives on the next street over the boy offered, "I can take you there." He took off running through a paved parking lot with Carl Brown in hot pursuit. I drove around the block and caught up with them right in front of the house. Hard to believe, but Ernest Carr was just approaching a little yellow cottage with white trim.

"Hey," Brown shouted, "You Ernest Carr?"

"Yes sir," was the reply.

"Y'all comere a minute, will you, we would like to talk to you," Detective Brown announced with his deep drawl.

The slender black boy walked slowly to the car.

"Jump in the back seat, will you, we'll only be a few minutes," Brown ordered.

It was easy to see the kid was a little frightened.

Ernest Carr was about six feet tall, probably weighed about one hundred fifty pounds, and was very light skinned. He was well groomed and neatly dressed, a good looking kid. When he opened his mouth he gave away the whole thing, with his feminine moves and dialect. I thought to myself, this kid is a three dollar bill if I ever saw one.

Detective Brown began asking questions.

"Yes sir," Carr responded to Brown's question, "I got picked up at Union Station in downtown Providence.

Union Station was an old, seldom used railroad station. A known hangout for homosexuals. Over time, I learned that Stanley Jendzejec knew where many of the haunts were.

Ernest continued to tell us that the man had a blue '67 or '68 Chevrolet.

"I was walking round in the train station and he asked if I wanted to go for a ride. So, I went with him. He took me over the state line into Massachusetts and we pulled into a rest area. There were a couple of other cars there. The guy was pretty big and I knew I had better not give him any trouble. He began rubbing my leg and then started rubbing my penis and got it hard."

"He asked me if I would blow him but I told him, 'No, I don't do that'. He bent over and took my penis in his mouth and gave me a blow job. He made me come off in his mouth. Then, he pulled my pants down and told me to turn around with my back to him, so I did. I was still scared," Carr added.

"Well sir," Carr continued, "He tried to stick his penis in my rectum and that's when these cops came up and shined a flashlight in the car". Carr went on, "I knowed I was in trouble, but this big guy said, 'Don't worry about it,' cause he said he was a cop too and showed me a badge".

"What happened then," we asked?

"The guy was outside talking with the cops, then, he got back in and said, 'See, I told you not to worry about it. It's alright'. He started the car and drove me back to the train station, or near it, and dropped me off. I got out and that's all there was to it".

After several more minor questions, we asked if Ernest Carr would give us a written statement and he readily agreed. I thanked him for being so candid and bid him farewell. I thought that was the end of Ernest Carr. I was wrong. We would talk with Ernest again.

With the statement in hand we travelled back to our town. I showed the statement to Art Capaldi and Senator Fecteau. No one seemed to know what to do with it, and it appeared the entire incident would die a quiet death. I was really getting tired of being wrong! There were no quiet deaths concerning anything in my town.

CHAPTER 26

Every day I worked, I felt I needed to concern myself with improvements to the police department. Not once did I ever lose my focus. By having a better equipped, more highly trained police department, the better service and protection we could offer the public. Truly, I cannot remember asking for a single thing that benefited me personally. I was doing political favor after political favor and didn't like it one bit. I was becoming a common police chief, but, I recalled only too vividly, what happened to Frechette, and how he was dumped and disgraced. Stanley knew he could get along without Frechette, so it was no big loss. Was I next?

When I was a state trooper, another trooper and I developed the state's first "no fix" traffic ticket. We knew it was encouraged by the colonel. I should have learned something from that too, but didn't.

We submitted our draft for the ticket through proper channels. It finally wound up with the major or state police executive officer, who thought it might not be a bad idea to tell the colonel he wrote it. No mention was made of me or Chuck Joyal.

What do you do, go to the state police executive officer and challenge him? Not if you like your job. Major George Weeden had already gotten one of my classmates terminated. This time Corporal Joyal and

I remained smart and silent while the major basked in the limelight of his significant contribution to the betterment of the Rhode Island State Police. See, you can carry a gun and still be unscrupulous.

It was very obvious that a vote, or potential vote, was more important to the politicians than a properly issued ticket. I was still burning after the lessons Frechette and Jendzejec taught me, when I wouldn't fix the bathing beach speeding ticket. By the way, I did not mention when they couldn't get me to fix that speeding violation, the motorist did have to appear in court. The town solicitor spoke with the judge in chambers before the arraignment and had the charge dismissed. Score one more for the bad guys.

The politicians didn't like to use the word "fix". They preferred "political consideration". I will admit there were a couple of times when "political consideration" was warranted. There were times I felt it was within my scope of responsibility and reasonableness to reduce a speed or change it to a warning, but as I noted previously, it was always with the knowledge and agreement of the issuing officer. Sometimes when the offender had no money and couldn't pay a traffic fine and the person was not a constant offender and had no record. We made a friend for the department even though our illustrious attorney general later accused me of altering court documents and tearing up court warrants. I never once did that. He could offer any unsubstantiated charge he wanted, and there was nothing anyone could do. A judge is the only one who can rule otherwise.

I did become involved in an incident far more serious than a traffic violation, one that was to come back and haunt me in months to come.

As usual, I was working one evening when young officer Tom Jones came into my office. Tom told me he had just taken a complaint report from a young housewife. It was reported that her nineteen year old sister had been molested in a doctor's office. I learned the basic facts and asked Tom to invite the two females to my office as soon as possible, and we would look into the matter further.

Officer Jones returned to my office with the two females. I asked Tom to remain during the interview. The older sister was in her late twenties, and was married to a very good friend of mine from years past. She introduced me to her sister, a slender, very attractive and fairly well proportioned brunette.

The younger girl explained she had an appointment with a local doctor earlier in the day for an examination. She didn't say what the examination was for, but did say the doctor told her the problem was mostly emotional and although he was not a psychiatrist, he thought he could help her. The girl's boyfriend had dropped her at the doctor's office, and would come back for her later, as treatment was going to take several hours. The young lady was led into an examining room by the doctor. No one else was in the office this particular day. The young lady was told to lie down on the examining table. She was fully clothed. The doctor explained to her he was going to give her a shot of sodium pentothal. She would likely become drowsy and once the drug took effect he would be able to extract inner emotional information she possibly had locked inside of her subconscious. The doctor administered an injection. Moments later she became drowsy and presumed she went to sleep. She went on to say that when she woke up she was still quite groggy. She had no idea how long she had been under sedation. She looked down and noticed the front of her dress was unbuttoned and her breasts were exposed. She looked beyond herself and saw the doctor standing in front of her. He had his penis exposed and was holding it in his hand. She closed her eyes again and felt the doctor sucking on her nipples. She stated she was too groggy and dazed to fully realize what was happening. When she made an attempt to ask him, the doctor told her to lie back down and relax because he was examining a growth on the back of her shoulder. She did have a growth that was treated earlier by the same doctor. The next thing she remembered, she was fully clothed and waiting in the outer office for her boyfriend to pick her up. The young girl was driven to her older sister's home where she went in and laid down. She still felt as if she was under the effects of the drug. When she awoke she related her experiences to her older sister who became alarmed, and with good reason. The older sister decided to make a formal complaint. I knew the doctor personally. I had known him for years, and went to him a couple of times myself for something minor. I had never heard of anything like this happening before.

On another occasion, a young wife came to the police station with a story about her fourteen year old brother. The woman was an army wife whose husband was stationed at a local Nike site. Supposedly, this same lad had been under treatment by the same physician. After several visits, the boy went to the office for a private examination. During our interview the young lad said the doctor gave him a shot of sodium pentothal, much in the same manner as in the young girl's case.

The doctor told the boy to lie down on the examining table. A short time later the drug was taking effect. The doctor unzipped the boy's pants and pulled his penis out. The youngster stated the doctor was kissing his penis. He further noticed the doctor had exposed himself and was working his own penis back and forth. I immediately ordered my detectives to begin an investigation and follow up on this complaint and see what additional information they could come up with. When I felt we had enough information to make an arrest, our star witness ran away from home. We further learned the boy had homosexual tendencies and problems that did not involve the doctor. We learned this from his older brother and some school friends. We dismissed the investigation.

After a great deal of thought and considering the evidence, we felt the pieces began to fall into place. I was convinced there was some validity to the girl's story. I called our town solicitor, Art Capaldi and asked for a legal opinion. We contacted another local practicing physician who knew the doctor under investigation. He told us if it was agreeable to the complaining parties there was another way to handle this. I was very aware that if we charged the doctor he unquestionably would retain a good criminal attorney and discredit this girls story as mere speculation and drivel, while casting a shadow over her, and making her look like a common tramp or someone looking to file a law suit for money. I decided to listen to the doctor and see what he had to offer.

I learned there was a board of practicing physicians, four in all, who could nearly demand psychiatric analysis for one of their own. The suspected doctor would be put in a hospital until the treating psychiatrist informed the board that the he was well enough to return to practice. Arthur Capaldi listened intently, as did the town council president, who by now, had been advised of the complaints. Enough had happened in the town, and we did not need another problem to blow the lid off again. However, it was a main concern of mine to see that justice was done on the girls' behalf. We all decided it was best for the doctor to stop practicing and get the necessary help.

The following noon we all met at a summer camp several miles in the country. The camp was owned by one of the doctors who participated and was a member of the board. The doctor under suspicion was requested to be there. I picked him up at his office and we drove to the camp. I was present, as was Art Capaldi, two of my detectives and all four members of the doctors' board.

The doctor in question was not aware of the complaint or subsequent investigation. After hours of conversation, alternatives and co-alternatives, the telephone rang. The call was for me.

I quickly learned there was a serious fire at the home of the doctor we had under suspicion at the meeting.

His wife and children got out safely, but the interior and exterior of the home had extensive damage. News of this all but caused the doctor to go off the deep end. Who could blame him? The doctor seemed to have concrete knowledge of who was responsible for the fire. He was certain his eleven year old son started it. The boy had a lot of problems and was a Nazi worshiper wearing clothing and displaying Nazi swastikas, etc. Others thought the fire might have been started by a bunch of local tough guys who had some problems with the doctor's fourteen year old daughter. The doctor resided in another town, and I never did find out if anyone was found responsible for the fire. On top of everything else the doctor had a lot to deal with; most of it bad.

With the account of the fire, everyone knew the doctor was under a great deal of stress. I guess being a doctor doesn't make you immune to problems. Neither does being a police chief.

The doctor finally agreed to commit himself to a mental hospital in Providence. It was a state facility and not really up to date. At his request, I drove him to the hospital and stayed with him all through admission. It was a long day and night. I felt that the doctor and yes, an old friend was signing himself into "One Flew Over The Cuckoo's Nest." The place looked just like it and if you haven't seen the movie keep an eye on the old movie channels.

After months of confinement, the doctor was re-examined and pronounced fit to return to practice. Every step of the way, I was in touch with the young girl, her sister and the sister's husband. They were graciously satisfied at the way everything was handled, and that the young girl was spared any further mental abuse. Everyone seemed satisfied, everyone that is, except our old friend, the state's attorney general who decided to make quite an issue out of it. I was accused of hiding the reports of the incident and using my authority, as chief of police, for not properly prosecuting the doctor. In his eyes, the right thing turned out to be absolutely the wrong thing. After all was said and done, this weasel did a pretty good job ruining my career in law enforcement and life at the time. It was like no one else was involved. I thought I involved all of the right people, including the victim, and her family, but obviously that wasn't good enough for attorney general Richard Isreal.

CHAPTER 27

It was 1971 and I was 34 years old getting very close to 35. Things were running smoothly in all corners of the town. Everyone seemed to be getting along with everyone else and there was peace at last. I was having some problems with a councilman named Edouard Jacques. He didn't like me from the beginning and made no secret of his feelings. Jacques was a man in his late forties; tall, thin and balding with wire rim glasses and the personality of a cobra. He looked like a baby chicken and acted really regal. He was an insurance salesman and would go from door to door collecting his monthly insurance premiums. I knew of two very attractive young ladies who told me Jacques was constantly trying to put some moves on them, and would find excuses not to leave their apartments. One volunteered to make a statement that he was an annoying man hoping she would get rid of him. I did not want to get into the embarrassment game again nor would I bring myself down to his level.

Jacques was a rumor monger. He started several dandies about me, one of which I was not going to let lie without confronting him. This charge really had nothing to do with my being chief of police and it happened before I was ever considered for the position as chief. Allegedly, I was buying a home for a young blonde who I was going to keep as my mistress. He named the location and vowed all of the information was absolutely correct.

To some degree it was.

I did have a deposit on a home and looked at it with this blonde lady. She just happened to be my wife at the time. Furthermore, this had nothing to do with my hometown of Coventry, Rhode Island, as the house was just over the line in the city of Cranston. When I learned of this, I immediately withdrew my offer. I simply did not want to leave Coventry.

When this real estate mess rumor occurred, I stopped in to see Senator Fecteau. I was really pissed.

"I'm sick and tired of this vicious bastard," I started stammering.

The senator told me he had heard several rumors about himself that had been started and circulated by Ed Jacques, and thought it was a good time to have a council meeting to clear the air. The meeting was hastily called for that evening. It was unusual but there were no other meetings or events scheduled that night. Everyone was present, all five councilmen, the town solicitor, Art Capaldi, the senator and, of course, me.

We did not waste any time getting on Jacques. I will give Eddie Jacques credit for one thing. He admitted what he had done and offered to resign, if he was causing this much dissention among party members. The rest of the men talked him out of it because it wouldn't look good for the party. I was all for his resignation, but I kept my mouth shut. The bastard got off with a small bit of lecturing.

Even then, I knew if Jacques was ever in a position, he wasn't going to forget what I had done, regardless of his insincere smile. I could hear his tail rattling in his pants. He eventually got his chance and made good use of it. He got me, and he got me big time, but we'll come that. In the meantime, a really good councilman by the name of Reggie Mailoux (May-you), who was the town council vice president, resigned citing person reasons. Guess who gets the nod as his replacement? Yup, Edouard Jacques.

Several more months went by and there still hadn't been any problems to speak of. My police officers had improved one hundred percent and performed as real professionals right to the last man. One of my department members asked me if I had seen the Providence Journal about Stanley Jendzejec?

"No, I haven't read anything," I answered.

He handed me a copy of the newspaper. The paper read, "Coventry town official beaten and left unconscious on city street." He was found wandering around in a dazed condition. The Providence rescue unit was called by two unidentified women. Mr Jendzejec was reported to be in fair condition at the Rhode Island hospital.

I called Art Capaldi. I thought what the hell, he had been in on everything else.

Art answered his own phone.

"Art, did you read about Stanley?"

"Yes," was his only reply.

"What do you think?" I asked.

"I don't know," Capaldi replied.   "From what I can find out Stanley was at a town committee meeting and when he left he went to Albro's store on the Coventry/West Greenwich town line. The store is located just west of the hub of activity in Coventry and very near an entrance ramp to Interstate 95. The store was open later than most other small country variety stores.

Arthur went on, "I guess Stanley stopped for cigarettes and when he came out, there was a young guy standing by his car and asked for a ride to Providence. Stanley supposedly told the stranger he wasn't going to Providence. The kid then brandished a tire iron or something and told Stan to get into the car or he would belt him over the head."

Arthur continued, "Well, you know how Stan always professes to be a coward, so he got in. Apparently Stanley drove the kid to some intersection in Providence and the kid told him to stop the car. Just before the kid started to get out of the car Stanley made a grab for the tire iron, but the assailant pulled the weapon back and slugged Stanley across the nose."

Art finished with, "I called the hospital and was told Stanley had a broken nose and a cut on the top of the nose,"

"Was there any attempt at robbery?"

"Not that I know of."

"You want to take a ride to Providence to see Stanley and then go over to the Providence police department and see what we can learn?"

Arthur said he would be ready in a few minutes.

When Art and I arrived at the hospital, we found Stanley asleep. We didn't bother him and went over to the police department.

The Providence detectives couldn't add much to what we already knew.

I was troubled with the description Stanley gave of his assailant. Allegedly, his attacker was approximately five foot eight inches tall and on the slender side. This account was published in the Providence Journal newspaper. Stanley is well over six feet tall and weighs more than two hundred twenty pounds. Suspicions were aroused in countless minds. Considering the assailant had a tire iron, or some type of weapon, I would not be reluctant to say that this could reduce or increase the size of any man.

I didn't see Stanley again until he got out of the hospital several days later. In our first encounter I told him I would be happy to assign a couple of our men to work with the Providence detectives to see what they could uncover. He waved me off.

"Never mind," Stanley said. The Providence detectives are working the case and if anyone can find anything they will."

I agreed to a point, but I reasoned, if the attacker did confront him in the town of West Greenwich, only a few feet over the Coventry town line, perhaps our people could come up with some information that might help. I even offered to get involved myself.

With that remark Stan became very irritated and sternly told me to, "Back off." I didn't press the issue. It took some time, but I did learn the truth.

Truth is, I did do a little investigating and came to learn Stanley Jendzejec never went anywhere near Albro's store that night.

Needless to say, the rumors were flying. I often thought this was a miserable little gossip laden town and a lousy place to live. It seems people have nothing better to do than step on others when they are down. Over the years, experience would teach me that damned near all of America was like that. I've lived in enough towns and cities across the country to know "Rumors Rule".

However, in Stanley Jendzejec's case, there was reason to suspect there was another side to the story. Turns out, there was.

CHAPTER 28

A week or so after the assault on Stanley, he came into my office. I asked how the Providence detectives were doing with the investigation. He told me he was called in to identify some photographs or mug shots as they called them in police jargon. Stanley said he couldn't identify anyone. So much for that, I thought.

It was more than a year later when I found out why Stanley really went to the Providence detective bureau. What I did find out, left me a little surprised. He had some really large "gonads" to attempt some of things he did, and it was doubtful he could have accomplished these things without authority from someone who had sizable political influence in the community, as well as the state. I would have been hard pressed to consider it was Senator Fecteau.

I learned that Stanley had gone back to speak with the investigating Providence detectives of his own accord. He was never invited back to view "mug shots". Someone had opened the door for him. Who? I spoke with the detectives a short time after Stanley met with them. The detectives told me Stanley had asked them to drop the investigation because his political career wouldn't benefit from anymore adverse publicity and it would hurt his family. Stanley was asked by one of the detectives if there was more to it than just dropping the investigation for the reasons he stated?

"Why," Stan asked?

"Well," said one of the detectives, "We have the impression that you might be a little gay yourself and the complaint you gave us wasn't quite accurate."

Stanley stated he just wanted the investigation dropped.

"We'll drop it if you level with us," the detective pressed on. "Are you queer?"

"I guess you hit the nail on the head," was Stanley's answer.

I saw the last page of the report myself. "Closed with exception." There wasn't much doubt in my mind what the exception was. Here was a guy, Jendzejec, who pushed Al Frechette out of the town's political picture, ruined his reputation and literally drove him out of town, and he himself turns out to be a homosexual. Add to this Stanley's molestation of a 17 year old lad from Providence, and we have a pedophile. Least of all, he skated again, with no charges from the Providence police department for filing a false police report. The filing of a false police report is a crime but not a soul touched it, including our illustrious attorney general Richard Isreal. Yup, Stanley Jendzejec had some juice.

It's one thing to suspect someone of something, but as a police investigator, you are never quite convinced until the cold hard facts are presented in their true light. That light couldn't have been much brighter in this case.

My take on this is that Stanley did pick someone up and made some moves on his passenger just as he did with Ernest Carr, the young black kid. The guy wasn't buying into the homosexual scene and beat the hell out of Stanley and left him lying on the sidewalk. As I explained, Stanley never went anywhere near that small country variety store that night and concocted the entire story also. The providence detectives didn't buy it and made him admit he lied but the political juice was on them and they made an intelligent decision to back off. Too bad I couldn't have learned from them. They saved their careers.

So let's stipulate that Stanley was no worse off for his actions. There was no real danger of him hurting anyone other than himself and perhaps his family. I hear that from ultra liberals who tell me they have some gay friends and they don't hurt anyone.

Really! Want to turn your four or five year old over to them for maybe a camping trip or a weekend alone?

I was involved in the arrest and prosecution of one case that still makes the hair stand up on the back of my neck. I was a state trooper then. After I relate this story, you examine your thoughts and tell me none of those people could possibly hurt another, maybe your child or a relative. Tell me how you are so sure they are such nice and good people? I am not on a gay bashing campaign, but I do caution, know who you are dealing with.

My supposition is there is a distinct possibility that a man who is homosexual can easily slip into a period of stagnancy where he, more or less strikes out in local circles but fails to connect with another member of his persuasion. He has a dire need to seize upon someone, to release his inner anxieties and no one is available at that moment. What happens when a juvenile, nine, ten or eleven years old is walking along the roadway and this "gay blade" offers the youngster a ride. A nice clean looking, well dressed man in a shiny automobile offers the youngster a ride. What harm, the young lad determines and gets in the car?

My first-hand knowledge of homosexual activities was extensive. Let me take you on a ride.

While a state trooper, I was on patrol in the Portsmouth/Middletown area right outside of Newport, Rhode Island. It was mid-afternoon and I got a radio message from my barracks dispatcher to be on the look-out for a Good Humor ice cream truck coming out of Newport and heading in my direction. The driver was suspected of molesting two young people. Handle with caution. I headed in the direction of the coordinates given and spotted the ice cream truck headed into a local neighborhood.

The ice cream truck was rolling along at perhaps fifteen miles per hour with bell jingling doing what it is supposed to do. Little children were running out to the sidewalks in front of their homes to await their treat for the day. I radioed my location and asked for some local backup or another state police cruiser, if there was one available. There was not. I pulled past the truck, put on the flashing red light and cut the driver off. I saw a look of horror on this guys face and that told me what I needed to know. I had the right guy.

A young man in his early twenties was operating the truck. Reportedly, earlier he was able to coax two other children into the truck. The boy was seven years old and his sister was eleven. The Good Humor man drove them fifteen miles to a wooded area. He bound the young girl to a tree and tied the brother to another tree. Then he proceeded to sexually assault the girl. When he finished with her, he tried to strangle her with a shoelace while the brother watched in horror. Finally, giving in to the boy's screams he stopped attacking the girl and concentrated on the boy. The perverted bastard assaulted the young boy. He bit and chewed on the boy and did other torturous things to him. It was quite a mess. I never did know for sure how the children faired, but I understood they were doing well after hospital treatment and probably professional counseling.

The accused had a wife and two young children. Remind you of anyone? Stanley was married with a couple of children.

In another case, I had what I thought was a good friend. He was a single man in his early thirties, was a local television personality, and worked for a Providence television station. I was married to my second wife at the time. The marriage was rocky, at best, and this incident didn't help the situation any. He seemed perfectly normal to all of us, but it became apparent, he was a perverted pedophile.

He spent quite a bit of time at the house, ate with us, rode in the cruiser with me and other troopers from time to time. He even presented me with a beautiful dog, a boxer. In conversation, we learned he did some free lance photography work for a downtown Providence department store. Nothing wrong with that! He asked if my wife's oldest boy could do some clothes modeling for him on a Saturday morning so he could do a photo shoot. That, too, was agreeable.

We came to learn a few weeks later that this alleged friend had my step-son modeling bathing suits. He was forced to change in front of him and was groped throughout the session. When we asked why he didn't tell us sooner he said he was ashamed and scared.

By now the man had transferred to a network studio in New York City. I called him and threatened the hell out of him, but to save the boy any further disgrace and embarrassment, I did not contact New York authorities. I regret that now, but the young man moved on with his life and has done very well for himself. I don't know what happed to the homosexual pedophile, but I will never forget him.

Most of us will never know what goes on in a victim's mind. Will the incident ever be washed away? Do we care? Probably not, unless it happens to someone close to us.

Most policemen care. That's what we got paid for. That's what our oath of office means: to protect and defend.

Now, is it possible that Stanley Jendzejec would contemplate or even consider the effects of his actions.

I think not. He was one of the town's leading citizens. Good church going man. Good family man. Civic and political stalwart. A man to be looked up to and respected. If anyone dared to threaten his dynasty, like the local police chief, he would be dealt with. Stanley and his henchmen would gather their forces and do what had to be done. If it was done properly, you could even get the state's attorney general to coerce a grand jury into indicting the chief of police on a criminal charge of extortion.

Mr. Crimebuster was really reaching with the extortion charge, considering there was no such criminal charge in the state statutes, and that decision was rendered by a superior court judge.

By then, the damage was done. When I was charged and the news was released to the media it made headlines all over the state of Rhode Island and beyond. When the judge threw the charge out, the media printed a small quarter column story close to the back of the newspaper, right next to the obituaries. Television and radio never even touched it.

CHAPTER 29

One evening in early 1972 I was out with a friend who owned a very popular restaurant and night club in town. His place called "The Showboat" was right on a lake. The building was literally shaped like a small cruise ship and had been there for years. My friends' father, a former professional wrestler, built the "boat" many years earlier and it was a local landmark. My friend, Norman Blair, and I went out to listen to a couple of show bands he was possibly interested in hiring to entertain at his club. We visited several night spots offering this type of entertainment. Neither of us had a drink. Several hours later we returned to the Showboat. I was sitting at the end of the bar talking with Norman. A man I knew as George Carter, a former Pawtucket, Rhode Island police officer sat down next to me.

Carter asked me what I was drinking and offered to buy me a drink. I told him I had a glass of tonic water and thanked him anyway. Carter left the Pawtucket police department under a cloud. He had applied for a position with my department but after a background investigation I was advised Carter was big trouble and probably wouldn't want him on my department. We declined his application.

Everything seemed fine. I said good night to my friend, Norman, excused myself and went home to bed.

I got home from the Showboat and Tom, who was still bunking at my house, came in a short time later. He said good night and went to bed. About one thirty in the morning I was awakened by the telephone. George Carter was on the other end and told me he needed to talk to me about some important information he had obtained that would cause me a lot of problems unless I could head them off before they became public. He would not tell me over the telephone what the information was. I told Carter I would meet him at my office. Carter said his wife and daughter were home alone and he couldn't leave them. Could I come to his house?

I didn't like the smell of any of this, but I finally relented and told him I would be over in a few minutes. One mistake I made was turning down Tom Jones' offer to come with me. Tom spoke out from his bedroom after overhearing the conversation, or at least my side of it. Tom asked if I wanted him to come with me?

I said, "No, get some sleep I'll be back. I can handle this."

My head kept telling me this was trouble, but I went anyway, mainly because I didn't want any problems with this guy and I didn't want him accusing me of ignoring a citizen in need. Count me stupid.

I arrived at Carter's home about twenty minutes after his call. He met me at the front door and invited me in. He had a standard three bedroom ranch home, neat, clean and obviously well taken care of by his Japanese wife. His wife and daughter were in the kitchen when I got there and he ushered me to a small dining room table. The females were ordered to go into the bedroom and go to bed. Both obeyed instantly, but appeared scared and upset. I wondered what this was all about.

Mr. Carter offered me a cup of tea. I declined. He said how about a beer. I again begged off and told him I wasn't drinking. I sat at one side of the table and Carter took up a position on the other side of the table directly across from me.

I was thinking in the back of my head what the Pawtucket police chief said when he called me and said I had a couple of "bad apples" in my town. He went on to say Carter was nothing but trouble when he was on the Pawtucket department and his buddy, James Aspinwall, was just as bad. Aspinwall lived right down the street from Carter.

There is no question that I was being set up for what was about to happen, but I had a reason for going. To add to the situation there was another ex-cop living right next door by the name of Chris Vespia. No question he was in on this also.

I knew Carter and Aspinwall were both nut cases. The Providence Journal newspaper wrote on February 20, 1970 that these men were "No Strangers to Trouble." A lengthy article in the newspaper provided quite an investigative report of trouble both of these men caused the Pawtucket department.

Amazingly, the attorney general, Richard Isreal, stated on February 18, 1972 that he was broadening a preliminary investigation of the tangled affairs of the Coventry police department into a full scale probe of the "affairs of the town". Once again, I say "Bullshit". Isreal wanted his investigation to go in one direction and that was toward me. He had nothing, and he knew it, but he wouldn't quit. He was determined to get something on me. Think an attorney general, the top law enforcement officer in the state, can't be corrupt himself? Think he can't be fed a lot of bogus information and extract only what suits his purposes? Did he jump to conclusions? Is it possible that the more people in a command position that he could be credited with "bringing down" would help his bid to be governor? Wonder what he'd say if you asked him now. Truth is he got his ass kicked in his bid to become governor. Wonder if my case had anything to do with it? I certainly hope so.

Back at Carter's house we talked for quite awhile. I saw the conversion going nowhere. Why did I go, you might ask? I reasoned I went because I did not want him at a town council meeting mouthing off about how he called his police chief and the chief did not respond. I suspected I was walking into a trap and went anyway. I admitted, "Color me stupid." Why didn't I take Tom Jones with me? Big mistake on my part trying to be considerate of someone else's comfort.

Hearing enough, I finally said to Carter, "I haven't heard anything that damaging from you and I think it's about time for me to leave." "I see no reason to listen to any more complaints about passing you over for employment with the Coventry police department." With that, and before I could get fully out of my chair, Carter dove across the table and we both went flying to the floor. George Carter was a pretty big guy weighing well over two hundred pounds. The wooden chair I was sitting in broke into a hundred pieces and Carter was groping around my waist looking for my plain clothes revolver. I yelled at him and told him I did not carry a gun so he was wasting his time. I remember yelling out,

"For Christ sakes Carter, your wife and daughter are watching."

He growled back "don't worry about them" and told them to get the hell back in the bedroom.

At this point I shoved Carter off me, got up and headed for the front door. He got up off the floor while I fumbled with the lock on the door. I yanked the door open and was about to open the storm door that was also locked when he came at me again with a chair leg in his hand. I ducked his swing and we both flew back on to his couch snapping off the legs. Carter was down and I gave him as hard a punch to the ribs as I had left in me and momentarily knocked the wind out of him. I got up and threw my shoulder into the door knocking it open and breaking the glass all over his front steps.

I was in Carter's front yard now, and headed for my police car to call for backup and get this maniac under control and arrested. I just couldn't get to my car quickly enough, get it unlocked and climb in, when here comes Carter again still swinging the chair leg,

"Come here and threaten me will ya," He screamed. He was acting for the gallery.

I caught a glimpse of Chris Vespia, the former cop and Carter's neighbor come out of this house fully dressed. At this hour? I found that a little odd.

Vespia was standing next to his car in his driveway when Carter grabbed me by the throat again and started ranting about me trying to intimidate him and his family. I pushed Carter away and ordered Vespia to help me hold Carter back or I would have him arrested for failing to help a police officer. He complied.

In the meantime, as documented in the local newspaper, Vespia's wife was on the telephone screaming, "The Chief of Police is on my front lawn, drunk, trying to beat up my neighbor. That made the headlines.

To put a cap on this rotten incident, I looked down the street and here comes James Aspinwall at four o'clock in the morning. He lived several houses away and could not possibly have been bothered by the incident or noise. How about a telephone call from Vespia's house? You think?

When I got back to the station I had a warrant drawn for Carter's arrest on charges of attempted murder of a police officer, assault and battery. Carter was picked up and held for arraignment before a local district court judge. He pleaded not guilty and was held on $3,500 bail which he was able to post and was set free until a trial date was set.

I knew Carter was put up to the assault, but I was never able to find out who put him up to it. My best guess was that Stanley Jendzejec was involved in this mess somehow. There was a very complicated and tangled web unfolding and I didn't have a lot of help untangling it.

On the day of Carter's trial in district court, I met with acting town solicitor Al Difiori and wondered why he was prosecuting this offense as assistant, (part time,) town solicitor and not Art Capaldi? He told me he was handed the case and that was it. No, truth is I suspect my good friend, Art Capaldi, was ducking any involvement with me. He was one of many who ran as far and as fast as he could go. He cast his lot to remain on the side of the councilmen, and especially Eddie Jacques, rather than be associated with me. No question in my mind Capaldi was advising the council all along in their endeavor to get rid of me. This was my good friend; this was the man I liked and had a good deal of faith in. No question, he was ducking. I wonder how he feels about that?

Because I smelled a rat immediately when I got to the courthouse, I told Al DiFiori I did not want to testify in the Carter thing and wanted all of the charges dropped. What did I have to gain? The judge got really angry when DiFiori told him what I wanted. I also knew there was nothing the judge could do to forbid me from dismissing this.

The judge started to berate me until finally I fired back at him,

"Judge, I have just received word that the Kent County Superior Court judge has upheld my firing as chief of police." I have no job and my career and reputation have been ruined." I have also been informed I have been indicted by the superior court on a charge of extortion (blackmail). About two hours ago the family court just granted my former wife a divorce."

I continued heatedly, "All of this has happened on the same day and now I am to testify before this court being represented by a part time assistant town solicitor, who doesn't even come from my town, before a judge I don't know and have never heard of. I've been set up enough, Judge, and you can get as mad at me as you want, hold me in contempt, or do whatever it is that you do, but I am finished with this."

The judge just looked at me, hung his head and said, "Very well."

That was that.

As I was leaving the courthouse, I saw George Carter across the street and wanted to run over and rip his head off his shoulders, but that certainly wouldn't have done any good.

Oh, and my good friend Norman Blair, was in court and begged me not to have him testify. I needed him to corroborate the fact that I was not drinking alcohol on the night Carter assaulted me. So much for good friends, huh? I never saw Norman again. I'm sure that pleased him just fine. Word was he was already sucking up to the new chief.

By the way, Norman must have pissed someone off big time because The Showboat was burned to the ground. Glad I was living in New Hampshire at the time.

The end result, and the last I ever heard of Carter, was that he filed a civil law suit against me. He sued me for $70,000. It was never clear to me why he sued. After initial notification of the suit I never heard anything else and assumed everything was dropped. I was told Carter moved to the city of North Providence where he had an altercation with a local police officer, and spent the night in jail. Later, I heard that Carter had died.

PART THREE

CHAPTER 30

Other than a little part time work here and there I had no job and no money. My two children were visiting from Florida where they lived with their mother. We were at my mother's house one evening and my daughter told me they did not want to go back to Florida. They had decided they wanted to live with me full time. My son was sitting right beside her and echoed the same sentiment. I just held my breath. I had no idea how I was going to take care of or support them. I do know that through all of the miserable circumstances that had taken place in the past few years, all the bitterness, loneliness and tears, I was one happy man. There is a God, I thought. I told them they had to call their mother in Florida and tell her of their decision. Patty called her immediately and the call ended quite well. Their mother said she would ship what clothes they had.

I had a third child from my second marriage, but Lisa's mother would never give her up, although she kept threatening to throw Lisa out. She liked dangling her custody over my head and needed her for leverage. There is a whole lot more to that part of my life but better left for another time.

Among my many endeavors to put bread on the table, I started a small real estate office in the neighboring town of West Warwick. Remember Joey Muschiano, the young barber? He was my partner. We rented a store front, leased some office furniture and went to work. Joey was pretty good at real estate in his semi-gangster approach. I wasn't very good at it and that was probably because I hated it.

One day Joey and I met a young father and his wife at a property. The "Lookie Loos" had been working with Joey for some time trying to find a house. Joey just couldn't get this man to make a commitment to buy a property. We went to a brand new home out in the country and waltzed him around the house. The young man started to hem and haw. Joey apparently had had enough and walked right up to within an inch of this guys face. In his best Robert DiNiro imitation, Joey squinted his eyes and blurted out,

"Hey, you got any money wit choo?"

The young man went pale and weakly replied,

"Yah."

"Lemme see it," Joey said in his best Italian enforcer voice.

The guy pulled a small wad of bills out of his pocket and held them up for Joey to see. In one swift motion Joey swept the bills out of the man's hand and said, "You just bought a house, follow us back to the office so we can get an offer typed up. You hear me?"

"Unh yah," the potential buyer replied, "I'll meet you there".

"Damn right you will," Joey added, "And I don't want any more bullshit out of you either". Talk about Raging Bull.

I told Joey, on our way back to the office, he should be more discreet with these people. He shouldn't treat them like hoods and punks, even though he fashioned himself as one.

"Screw him," Joey replied. "He'll be there. I got his money in my pocket."

I couldn't believe he had done that. There were a thousand Joey stories to relate, just like that one. By the way, the guy did come to the office, signed an offer to purchase and bought the house. I even made a couple hundred dollars on that deal.

One might wonder what these stories have to do with the Coventry police department. Just want you to know who we were dealing with here. Keep in mind I was still hanging on the extortion charge.

Joey and I went out one night and wound up at The Showboat. The two of us were sitting at a table out in the lounge having a beer. Suddenly, Joey hurriedly got up from the table and took off. He was out of sight in a flash. A moment later, I got up and went looking for him. I walked by another table where two females were sitting. One of these women was a former flame of Joey's, and believe me he had plenty of them. As I walked by, I asked if they knew where Joey was. Gloria told me she didn't know, but he was acting like a real asshole.

I replied, "What's new?"

I checked in the kitchen and learned Joey had left with somebody who was giving him a ride home. Truth is, Joey got drunk and Norman Blair, the owner, threw him out. Joey wound up at the police station charged with something, I don't know what. He was going to be held overnight. I was able to speak with my old desk sergeant and asked if they would release him to me.

I figured I would just drive Joey home. They agreed. I took Joey home and that was that.

A few nights later there was a knock on my front door. I was at home with my two children. When I opened the door, two of my former police officers were standing there. One of them was Gerry Rondeau. He and I grew up together. You could tell he was upset with what he had to do, and he explained he had a warrant for my arrest. It had been sworn out and could I please come to the police station with them? Gerry explained they had a complaint from Gloria that I had threatened her when I asked where Joey was and Chief Pajak signed the warrant, and directed them to pick me up. A friend of mine was at the house visiting and I asked if he could take the kids to my mother's while I was gone. He said he would. I doubt they had any idea what was going on.

There was no doubt in my mind who was behind this. I found out later I was absolutely right. Richard Isreal. Somehow word of the incident at The Showboat got back to Pajak. He contacted the attorney general's office asking how to handle the complaint. Our illustrious attorney general had Gloria interviewed and got her to admit that I said something like "I'll blow up your house." A few days after I was arraigned, Joey talked to Gloria and asked what happened. She said Pajak and "They", whoever they were, badgered the hell out of her until they got her to say I had made the threat. Truth is, I never made any such comment Joey did. Joey had a volatile temper, especially when he had a few in the gut, drinks that is. It took Joey a long time but he finally admitted he had a drinking problem and got cleaned up.

Gloria deserves a lot of credit because she went back to the attorney general and told them she was upset and blamed me for what Joey had said. Isreal was pissed off and threatened to charge her with making a false report. In the end, he had nothing and instructed Pajak to drop the charges. To my credit, and due to a few friends in the media, the newspapers and television didn't touch the story. That incident was over, too.

With all my education, background and practical experience, surely someone, somewhere, needed a highly trained, skilled practitioner in the field of law enforcement; security perhaps. There had to be someone out there that would appreciate my qualifications and offer me a job. Bullshit!

My oldest brother died of a massive heart attack at the age of thirty nine. Some years later, his widow Margie, befriended a man who was a small local contractor. His name was Gene Renfret. He offered me a part time job helping him frame houses. I jumped at the offer that paid four fifty an hour. Money was money and it was honest money. Physically, I had never worked that hard. By the time I got home at night my rear end was so sore I couldn't even sit down, but I got broken in. In three days Gene and I had a house ready for the electrical wiring and inside finish. These were average twelve hundred square foot slit levels. Gene was a working madman and I did my best to keep up with him.

I also had two of the greatest friends anyone could ask for. Bob and Patsy Kettell ran a fruit and vegetable market quite close to the main gate at Quonset Point Naval Air Station. They worked extremely hard and did quite well until President Nixon decided to close the naval facility in the early 1970's. The entire area dried up and the military families moved. Thousands of people were badly affected. Many folks just boarded up their windows and walked away. The area and related services were devastated. Word was that's what you get Rhode Island, when you don't vote for Nixon in the general election. Nixon also closed the long established Newport Naval base with the same devastating effect on the residents and businesses surrounding it.

Prior to the closing of Quonset Point, Bob and Patsy offered me a portion of their land to put a small discount center on. A man, who was a friend of a friend of mine, donated two older cabins to use as the retail store. Remember those before motels? He moved the small buildings to the spot Bob and Pat offered (no rent charged either) and joined them together for the store. I sold eight track tapes, small radios, some cheap watches and other trinkets. The navy guys loved my little shop. They could buy items cheaper from me than at the PX (post exchange). All of my goods came from Frank "Babe" Kowal, another friend of many years. Babe would let me take from his store what I thought I could sell on consignment. I would pay him after I sold the product and keep my small markup. I never made much but I did bring home a few extra dollars.

I worked with Gene Renfret in the morning framing houses and would race to my store in early afternoon and work until early evening. My daughter, Pat, helped a great deal. One important thing came out of all of this. We were sharing happy times.

I have said it a thousand times, "My kids saved my life back in those days." I didn't have time to go out or fool around or do much of anything else. I spent a lot of hours at home with the kids who I absolutely adored and still do.

Many said Babe dealt in stolen goods, but everything I had from him came with a legitimate invoice. Babe was good to me and I always appreciated his help. Many years later, and no one seems to know why, Babe was shot in the head. Executed is a better description since he had five thirty-two caliber bullets in his head. The crime was never solved. All of the local cops and professional people dealt with him.

During the time that Bob and Patsy operated their fruit stand, they got to know every state trooper that passed through the Wickford Barracks state police area. They were good to all the guys and always had a smile, a practical joke and a bag of goodies for them to take home.

Bob was quite an athlete and played a lot of baseball and softball. As we grew older Bob sponsored a semi-fast pitch softball team and a number of the players were state troopers. Bob was the team's star pitcher. It seems I was the team's star batter. I won three batting titles and Bob's team won three championships. To this day, Bob and Patsy are loyal Yankee fans. No, better said fanatical Yankee fans.

I remember, when we were in our late teens, a bunch of neighborhood kids would jump in Bob's old lime green 1950 Ford and drive to a small hill on our street. The hill was the only place we could pick up the Yankee game broadcast. He never had any gas in his car and we were always pushing the damn thing back to the Torino Social Club (the club was an old neighborhood hangout) parking lot. Bob would attempt to scrounge enough money, or we all chipped in, to buy a jug of gas and get going again. Man that was good fun.

Between friends like Bob, Patsy and Babe, I realized there were good people out there and that gave me hope. I was determined not to let my children down. I would give them every ounce of blood, sweat, and yes, tears to help us survive. We did!

A year and a half after I was fired, there still had not been a decision from the superior court judge, Anthony Giannini on the extortion charge. It was a long wait.

Another friend I grew up with was Tony Cipolla Don't know where he got his nick name, but we all called him Chipper. He was a really good guy from a very nice Italian family.

One day while I was at the real estate office, Mr. Cipolla, Chipper's, father was walking down the sidewalk in front of the office. Mr. Cipolla didn't drive a car and as he got to the office door, I was standing in the entrance and Tony, Sr. stopped to say hello. I asked how he was doing and shook his hand.

He replied, "I'm good, how you doing?"

"I'm OK, just trying to scratch out a living and take care of my kids. You know how that goes," I said.

Mr. Cipolla looked at me and asked if I had heard anything from superior court yet.

"No, not yet."

"Ya know," he said, "Judge Giannini and I are pretty good friends." We're in the Knights of Columbus together".

My ears perked up as I stood there listening.

Tony, Sr. went on, "You're a really good man and I have known you since you was a kid. You really got screwed by the politicians and I didn't like it. I would like to talk to him about you if that would be OK?"

I didn't know what he could do since trying to reach one of these guys was like trying to talk to God.

"Sure," I replied, "I would just like a decision one way or the other. I need to make provisions for my children."

"Ok, you be good and I'll see what I can do," he said as he waved and walked off.

I don't have any way of knowing, but old Tony Cipolla dragged up a miracle from somewhere because within a week I was notified by my attorney, John Tramonti, that Judge Giannini agreed with his assertion that there was no such charge as "extortion" on the books in the State of Rhode Island. Essentially, the attorney general fabricated the charge and I had done absolutely nothing wrong. I was off the hook and it was over. I could now start thinking about getting on with my life. Only problem was, it was way too late to chase after my job as the chief. Thank God for small miracles and friends in the Knights of Columbus.

CHAPTER 31

With everything that had happened I knew I was not going back to law enforcement and I saw no future in and around Coventry, Rhode Island. Thinking about it long and hard, it was time to make a decision and move on. But where? My general contractor gig (we had a small construction company) and real estate office with Joey all ended and at this point had no employment prospects. I applied for a position with what was billed as the world's second largest management and consulting company. The company had sales people and consultants all over the world. They hired me and I was sent to Des Plaines, Illinois for several weeks of training. When training was complete, I was assigned to Northern New England, Pennsylvania and New York City. Quite a challenge!

In the meantime I was offered an opportunity to interview with a police department in (believe it or not) Coventry, Connecticut. I thanked them for the offer but did not want to relocate my children at this time. They had been through enough. I was doing well with the consulting company but doing a lot of travelling. I was not happy with the travelling aspect of the job. I eventually accepted the fact that this company was not for me. In the meantime, I was transferred by the company to New Hampshire. I talked with the kids about it and Pat told me she could finish out her senior year in Coventry and stay with the next door neighbor whose daughter was one of her best friends. The Babcock's were really nice people. Michael didn't have a problem coming to New Hampshire with me. I began to think things were looking up. I decided to sell our home and move. It worked well for a time, but then the thought of leaving Michael while I was off travelling appealed less and less, so I decided to quit.

While I was still with the consulting company, one hot summer day in August of 1975, I decided to cut my business calls short. On my way home I stopped for a cold beer. Something I never did, especially alone, but this mid afternoon I did. There was a young thirty-ish man behind the empty bar. I learned his name was Ronnie. The building started out to be a Seven-Eleven that never took off. It was turned into a small restaurant and lounge. Quite nice!

I was preparing to leave when I off handedly said to Ron, "If you ever need a bartender, let me know."

I was amazed when Ronnie asked if I could start tomorrow. Holy crap, I thought. Ron told me he was splitting duties with another man and really needed someone he could count on. I was stuttering and stammering wondering "what have I done"? Before I knew it, I had said yes, but also added, "I have to be honest with you, I have never really worked behind a bar, but I can learn".

Ronnie replied, "You come in tomorrow and I'll work with you for awhile, you'll pick it up quickly". Ron went on to tell me there was a very simple drink book on the shelf behind the bar that would tell me how to make about any kind of drink and also had a picture of the type of glass to pour the drink in. What a savior that little book was.

One day, shortly after I started, a guy came in with his wife or lady friend and ordered a Pink Lady. I had no idea what he talking about and couldn't find it in the drink book. About all I knew was the drink was red and made in a shaker. I thought, "oh, screw it" and made a bloody mary. The guy looked at me and said,

"That ain't no Pink Lady!"

I replied, "It's very close to pink, I'm having a tough day, so just shut up and drink it".

The young man just hunched over and said, "Oh, OK, thanks".

I heard him tell his companion, in hushed tones, "That guy's crazy". They left shortly thereafter. I was in for a few years of fun and relaxed times as I tried to get my head back on straight.

Matter of fact, one evening a lady walked in alone and sat at a table against the partitioned wall just across from me. Holly, my cocktail waitress, ordered a Kahlua and milk drink. I made the drink and asked Holly if she had ever seen that girl before. Holly replied, "No".

I told her, "When you deliver this drink, tell her I am going to marry her".

Holly never told her but that didn't matter, because about a couple of years later I did marry the girl and have been out of mind in love with Dianne for more than 35 years.

Keep in mind she is one of the editors of this book. Thanks, hon.

My son graduated from high school and went almost immediately into the Marine Corps. Like father, like son. He has made me proud. Patty went with Donna Babcock to Florida on her senior trip. She met a guy, Bill Edmonson. She came home to tell me she was going back to Florida to see spend some time with Bill.

"Why," I asked?

"Because we are going to be married," Pat said.

I was crushed, but I also knew my daughter had a mind of her own and if she thought Bill would make her happy then I would not stand in her way. They married and produced my first wonderful grandson, Joshua.

Unfortunately, their marriage ended a few years later. That pained me a lot. On the other side of the coin, Patty decided to move to California and lived with Dianne and I for awhile which allowed us to reconnect and spend lots of time with our grandson.

* * *

A little side story; Coventry high school tradition-ally had a senior class day and some of the students got voted to be a town official for the day. They shadow the department head for the day and are taken to lunch and then a party at "The Showboat" that night.

After the kids had voted, it turned out that Pat was selected to be the Chief of Police for the day. She got to spend an exciting day with Pajak who by now was the new chief. A little uncomfortable? Bless those kids, they got to stick it to Bozo Pajak and there was nothing he could do about it. Even the kids knew I took a hosing.

By the way, Pajak was only the chief of police for a couple of years when a new administration created a position of Director of Public Safety in the town. They held interviews and Pajak walked around in a daze for a short time wondering what hit him. Then he died. I think he was still in his fifties.

* * *

In New Hampshire, I had a part time auto detailing company and worked for several automobile dealers. My wife was managing an office for a welding company just outside of Manchester. I got a fairly good sized account from a Chevrolet dealer in Nashua, N. H. and hired a young man to work with me. One morning I went to pick him up and he told me he didn't want to do work that hard anymore and quit. I had all of these vehicles to clean, could make some pretty good money and suddenly no help.

Dianne had some time off from her office duties and said, "Can I help you?"

"Thanks, hon," I said, "But, this stuff will kill you, it isn't easy".

It was extremely hard work and very physically demanding and my dainty little wife would have some difficulty handling the things that had to be done.

"I can fill your spray and detergent bottles for you," she said.

"OK," I finally agreed and off we went to work.

I never looked back and to this day I can't believe what we (as a team) were able to accomplish.

The weather turned sour in November in New Hampshire and it was time to crash the business for a time. Di got another office job with a building contractor and worked a few days a week. I headed back to the lounge and was fortunate that my reputation apparently preceded me and I didn't have a problem getting a job. Unfortunately, it was "just a job" and I knew we could accomplish and deserved more and were willing to work hard for it.

CHAPTER 32

In 1978, Dianne and I were having a conversation about our future and I asked, "Where are there more cars in good weather than anywhere else?"

"I have a friend in California," she said, "Let me call Anita and see what it's like out there".

California, I thought, I've never been there.

To make a long story short, I was in Woodland Hills (Los Angeles), California ten days later.

I had an old beater of a 1967 Chevrolet station wagon with half the body rusted out from those New Hampshire winters. The detailing equipment amounted to a small power washer, some waxes and cleaning rags. I got a one bedroom furnished apartment in Encino in the San Fernando Valley right off the Route 101 freeway and a block north of Ventura Boulevard. It was about a 25 to 30 minute drive to downtown Los Angeles, Hollywood, and Beverly Hills. By the time I paid the first month and last month rent and security deposit, I had $400 dollars to my name and Dianne was on the way with Penny, our miniature Schnauzer.

I picked her up at the airport and we drove to our apartment. I stayed off the freeway all the way home and took what they called "surface streets." I told Di I just wanted her to see some of the scenery. Truth is I was scared to compete with the lunatics driving the freeways.

They took aim with their vehicles and I actually thought they were trying to kill me. Their favorite sign was giving the finger and they just loved that horn. Really!

We began our lives in California. Within a year we bought our first home on a VA loan and began to build our business. Dianne simply continued to amaze me. Truth is she still does.

Some eight years later we had a full blown detail shop and supported three more.

You racing fans will recognize the name of Andy Granatelli. He won the Indy 500 a couple of times and is the owner, founder of STP oil treatment and other well known products. We had a detail job to do for a girl who worked in the bank building where his offices were located. I was riding up in the elevator to pick up the keys to her Cadillac dressed in our company uniform work clothes. Our business name "The Car-tender" was embroidered on the right side of my shirt and my name, Harv, over the left pocket. I had on a matching dark blue baseball cap with another embroidered patch above the visor. Suddenly, I felt s light tap on my shoulder. I turned and an Italian looking, kind of short man weighing more than two hundred pounds was standing right behind me. He had dark hair and eyes. With a little practice he could have been a gangster. Robert DiNiro could have used him in one of his "tough guy" movies.

I smiled at him as he said to me,

"Who are you and what do you do," Granatelli asked?

I told him we owned a small automobile detailing (big in CA) company in Woodland Hills. In California, you are what you drive. It's definitely a status symbol.

"What are you doing here," Granatelli asked again?

There was nothing mean or malicious about him as I told him I was picking up the keys for a car from a girl that worked on the top floor.

"What's her name," he asked? I told him and he said, "Oh ya, she works for me".

He stuck his hand out and said, "I'm Andy Granatelli."

I told him I certainly knew who he was and what he did. He owned several businesses one being Tune-Up Masters where a person could bring in their car and have it tuned up in a matter of minutes. He was well-known and very successful.

He went on to say "If the cars you clean come out looking anything like you they must be beautiful".

Granatelli told me he would like to talk with me about my business. I told him he had better hurry because my wife and I were selling. Time to leave El Lay (Los Angeles.) He asked if I could meet with his son Antney. That's Italian for Anthony. Good thing I was brought up with Italians, among others. Granatelli said he might be interested in putting some detail shops in his Tune-Up Masters locations and would need someone to oversee the entire operation. He asked if I could come in the following day. I agreed because I wanted to see what he had to offer.

The following day I arrived at the big bank building and went up to the top floor. Anthony Granatelli, Jr. met me in the office lobby. We shook hands and he ushered me into his office. Anthony Jr. laid out the plan he and his father had discussed. He said they were seriously thinking about expanding into the auto detailing business and wanted to open a detailing shop at every one of their locations. Would I be interested? I didn't say anything, I just sat and listened. The hook came last.

Anthony, Jr. finished with, "We would require a five year commitment from you with an agreement to put our business plan in motion.

I didn't have to do too much thinking before I said, "I want to get out of the detailing business and I do not want to stay in Southern California, New Mexico or Arizona, so I will respectfully have to decline." I thanked him and his father for the consideration and hoped they would understand. I didn't want to tie up five years of my life with anyone.

We accomplished a lot and had a good life in southern California, but I sure did not want to spend our lives in this crazy environment. We met a lot of celebrities. Too many to mention here. We had a very good friend, still is, who got me involved in doing what they call industrial films. I was on Lifetime channel for a telethon once. I played a "know it all" bartender. Sound familiar? My wife always accompanied me to watch the filming and always wound up being an extra and got paid for it, too. She was just that cute; still is.

Eight years passed quickly and I had had enough of the fast paced life. We made a good living, but I think we both knew it was time to go. We sold the house and the business and headed to the Midwest where my wife's sister lived. They are so close you would think they are joined at the hip. Now it was time to carve out a new life and hope this was our last stop. It didn't start out well. There were meager jobs. Dianne went to work at a chiropractor's office. I stayed home and did some woodworking to take to trade shows, festivals and fairs. It didn't take long to realize what a "loser" that was. Everybody was doing woodworking and most, better than me.

We had gone through just about all of our money. Our first severe winter, we got a fuel oil bill for $200.00 and couldn't pay it. I was telling a friend out in California about our dire circumstances and that financially we were down and out. I didn't ask for anything, I was just venting. A couple of days later there was a $200. check in our mail box with a note, "we love you". We will never forget Frankie and Barbara Gould. Over the years, we have given that $200 to people in need numerous times and have done it in their names.

I've said many times, one of the happiest days of my life was watching the moving van go up the street with our belongings in it, headed for our new home.

We arrived in Wisconsin and bunked in with my sister in law, her husband and two kids. About a month later, we bought our first house in Wisconsin.

The sale of our business in California went sour and the young man that bought it decided he would rather party and go to the beach and so on. He never got the message. He needed to take care of business so business would take care of him. Four months after arriving in Wisconsin, I was headed back to California, took back what was left of the business and eventually re-sold it for next to nothing. In truth, we lost over $40,000.

I lived in the back of my pickup truck inside one of my garage bays until Frankie loaned me a camper trailer to put on the lot. At least I was close to work. I lived that way for four months.

So here we are in the Midwest with no money, again, and only my brother in law and sister in law to lean on. Mike, my brother in law, was an attorney who would eventually become a circuit court judge and spend sixteen years in that position before retiring. Dianne went to work for Mike as a legal secretary before he became a judge. He and his partners had a very well respected local law practice.

I was driving a propane gas truck and was offered a sales/marketing position by the company. Here I go again, travelling all over the Midwest. As with the consulting job, I hated being away from home five and one half days a week so I returned to delivering gas.

Our daughter remarried, and came out for a visit. After returning to California, she and her husband, Ken decided the Midwest would be a great place to bring up baby Bryan that was on the way. Pat, Ken, Josh, four cats and two dogs resided with us in our tiny two-bedroom cottage. Fun all around! It was like zoo-America. Pat and Ken decided it was time to look for a house. Dianne and I went out with them numerous times. I was astounded at the lack of interest the local real estate agents showed in them.

A light went off and I decided I needed a change in my life too.

That lack of interest caused me to go back to real estate school and see what I could make of it this time around. I quit the propane gas job, passed the test, got my real estate license and began selling houses.

No one thought we would make it around here, especially in the location we had. We did! When weather set in and it really got cold, the real estate brokers and sales people would literally hibernate. I didn't and went knocking on doors and talked to everyone. In the first month after the office opened we had Simmons Real Estate signs all over the town. Somebody was eating their words. After a few months, I had two other people working for me and eventually was successful in luring my wife away from a steady paycheck to come and run the business as she had always done. We were on our way in no man's land. Coming from Los Angeles, we were facing reverse culture shock, but we hung in there.

We did not have an abundance of friends but we were meeting people through the business.

One day a man I barely knew came into my office and asked if I did real estate appraisals?

"Sure," I said.

"Good," Terry Pfaff said. He was the vice president of a local bank. "We have been using one guy pretty regularly and I would like to spread the work around a little and thought you might like the business."

I almost jumped him. He told me he would be sending me some appraisal orders. Several days later, he did and I got an order for my first appraisal.

After Terry left my office I immediately called my wife and questioned, "What's an appraisal?" Then I explained what had happened. Once again, we never looked back.

Soon we needed more space and purchased a small older cottage, renovated it and turned it into a Century

21 franchise office. Dianne got her real estate license. I continued doing both real estate and appraisals. After several years, I suggested to Dianne that we should try to sell the real estate business and concentrate on expanding the appraisal business. We had interested buyers and sold the building along with the business.

There was a business rental available not too far from where we were located and the area was expanding. We were in the right place at the right time. After one year at this location, a building across the street came up for sale. I learned what I could from the owner and he agreed to accept my offer. We bought and renovated the small three room office building. It had three large garage bays attached to it. Plenty of storage. This building had everything we needed and served us well for twelve years. I really think a lot of people were surprised at what we had accomplished. We became very well known and respected in the industry.

I got involved in local politics and ran in a five way race for county supervisor. I wasn't given much of a chance. I won! The following term I won again and was elected by my fellow county board members as chairman of the board. Quite an honor and a ringing endorsement that we were starting to belong.

We sold our old two-bedroom home and moved to a very nice section of the township, just outside of the city. We have just about totally renovated this house. Even if I do say so myself it is our dream home set atop a small hill on two and one half acres of very pretty country property. My brother in law says it looks like a park up here. We have been here well over twenty years.

I know toward the end of this story, I may seem to take you on a family odyssey and it isn't completely related to "the Coventry story", but it is. I went from the depths of despair I thought I would never recover from to looking into the sunshine again.

Although I knew it was imperative that I move away from Rhode Island, it was difficult, at best, to leave friends and family. There was no future for us there and we had to build a life somewhere else. I just didn't know we would eventually end up in Wisconsin. I didn't know that I would ever again experience the "good life", but we have.

We have worked our little buns off, but we made it and we are proud of one another and appreciate those who have applauded for us. We have accomplished something positive and we are told, gained the respect of the community.

I was testifying in court regarding an appraisal case many years ago. The opposing attorney said something a bit negative that he felt I may have done.

The judge cut him off at the ankles and said, "I have known Mr. Simmons for years and his credentials and reputation are impeccable".

That was really something.

Dianne and I retired in December 2009 and we are comfortable and happy. We are both still in pretty good health and we are thankful and appreciate our good fortune.

The good Lord has been very gracious.

Thank you to all of our friends for the support you have given us over the years. We will never forget you.

The End

Made in the USA
Lexington, KY
18 March 2011